خطّ التّماس

THE GREEN LINE

خطّ التّماس

THE GREEN LINE

BY MAKRAM AYACHE

ARABIC TRANSLATION BY HIBA SLEIMAN

PLAYWRIGHTS CANADA PRESS

TORONTO

LIBRARY AND ARCHIVES CANADA CATALOGUING IN PUBLICATION
Title: The green line : khaṭṭ al-tamās / Makram Ayache ; translated by Hiba Sleiman.
Other titles: Khaṭṭ al-tamās
Names: Ayache, Makram, author. | Sleiman, Hiba, translator.
Description: Arabic characters in title transliterated. | Lines by Arabic-speaking characters have been provided in both English and Arabic. | In English with some Arabic.
Identifiers: Canadiana (print) 20240321189 | Canadiana (ebook) 20240325052
   | ISBN 9780369104922 (softcover) | ISBN 9780369104939 (PDF)
   | ISBN 9780369104946 (EPUB)
Subjects: LCGFT: Drama.
Classification: LCC PS8601.Y33 G74 2024 | DDC c812/.6—dc23

Playwrights Canada Press staff work across Turtle Island, on Treaty 7, Treaty 13, and Treaty 20 territories, which are the current and ancestral homes of the Anishinaabe Nations (Ojibwe / Chippewa, Odawa, Potawatomi, Algonquin, Saulteaux, Nipissing, and Mississauga / Michi Saagiig), the Blackfoot Confederacy (Kainai, Piikani, and Siksika), néhiyaw, Sioux, Stoney Nakoda, Tsuut'ina, Wendat, and members of the Haudenosaunee Confederacy (Mohawk, Oneida, Onondaga, Cayuga, Seneca, and Tuscarora), as well as Metis and Inuit peoples. It always was and always will be Indigenous land.

We acknowledge the financial support of the Canada Council for the Arts, the Ontario Arts Council (OAC), Ontario Creates, the Government of Ontario, and the Government of Canada for our publishing activities.

To Baba, who buried Lebanon inside his heart when he left.
To Mama, whose love reshapes and reimagines borders.

Pain travels through families until someone is ready to feel it.
—Steph Wagner

Come, return to the root of the root of your Self.
—Jalāl al-Dīn Muḥammad Rūmī

SO WHY DISTURB IT?

AN INTRODUCTION BY MAKRAM AYACHE

RAMI: Memory is a funny thing. So quiet if left undisturbed.
ZIDAN: So why disturb it?
RAMI: I don't know if I have an answer to that.

These lines came to me near the end of this play, but this question has been the seed out of which *The Green Line* was born. As I was writing this play, I kept asking how does intergenerational memory live in my body? Does it? How am I, a queer Arab who grew up in the prairies of Alberta, connected to my parent's experiences surviving a fifteen-year civil war in Lebanon?

Surely, we imprint onto one another, parents to children, and children to parents. In so many ways, this play was my yearning to be closer to my Arabhood. I could speak the language and my memories of Lebanon are only the charming summer days when the mountains stood still and Beirut was a renaissance of art, dancing, eating, and drinking. I have the immense privilege of walking across borders as if they were the swinging doors of a saloon. I took it all for granted when I went to Lebanon at fourteen years old, then again at sixteen, eighteen, twenty-two, twenty-six, and twenty-eight. I have cousins and kin who would dream of my mobility. But I have others who, even given all the world, would never leave their towns and cities in Lebanon.

Lebanon is a garden tended to by many hands. Some are forced to weed the soils and others would rather plant roses than fruit. Some would rather build homes in the cedars while others would rather chop them down to plant skyscrapers and condos. Her earth is watered by blood, maybe that's why her rocks are red. As I wrote this play, I kept asking, how does this soil live in my body? And somewhere between my search through intergenerational memory and the soil of this earth, I found answers that asked better questions.

My parents held a vision of Lebanon in their hearts and hands when they crossed oceans and settled into a small town in Alberta. That vision was given to us on the dinner plate, as mujaddara, koosa, hummus, and djej w roz. It was lovingly provided to us in the Arabic language, where they taught us to pronounce habibi, ya albi, ya omri, and to'borni with perfect accents. My parents made the deliberate decision to practise Arabic with us, so we maintain the language, at the cost of their English never becoming quite proficient. One of many sacrifices immigrant parents make. Lebanon was given to us in our values, held closely to our spine, we were a part of something ancient and permanent. Our community was axiomatic, for better or for worse.

In so many ways, I had to go back, through the terrains of the civil war, hearing the stories of my dad and mom, to plant myself in this memory. I learned of my mom finishing a law degree in the midst of the fractured militaristic landscape. I learned of my dad's efforts to maintain peace with the schism in his communities; he was a Druze Muslim person who grew up amongst Christians, his friends forcefully became enemies, a fact he wouldn't accept. And while so much of *The Green Line* is fictional, the emotional truth of how these wars live in our bones is consistent with the experiences I was taught and felt.

But I learned that intergenerational memory is porous. I wasn't only taking from them, but I would give. I was a queer boy, a little gay kid from as early as I can remember. And in writing this play, I walked through the pores of our memory in the opposite direction. In 2016 I went to Lebanon and explored queer life for the first time. To hear my people speak the words of queerness in our language, something was legitimized within me. This queerness did not only belong to the Western world. It was here and it was real.

Sometimes I think this play is about my reckoning with what Arabhood means to me. Sometimes I think it's a love letter to my mother and father. Sometimes, it's a poem to Beirut and my yearning to be part of everyone there. But most of all, I think this play is my attempt to dig a queer stake into the history of our memories. We are here now, and we were here then.

When I discovered images of the real Green Line carving through a civil-war Beirut, I was transfixed. The earth was screaming, tearing, and cleaving across a people who had lost their unity. It not only became a symbol dividing West Beirut from East Beirut, but it was a demarcation for the ways the war, immigration, memory, and queerness have all cleaved through my body and created divisions where divisions should not have happened.

Perhaps by disturbing the soils of memory I'm able to till this earth and make it fertile for new growth once again, one that reconciles all the disparate sides and brings the contradictions together in undiscovered and nourishingly new ways.

The Green Line was first produced by Downstage Theatre and Chromatic Theatre at the Big Secret Theatre, Arts Common, Calgary, in April 2022 with the following cast and creative team:

Mona: Sepidar Yeganeh Farid
Yara: Filsan Dualeh
Zidan / Fifi: Ryan Abd'u'llah Hooper
Rami / Naseeb: Makram Ayache

Director: Jenna Rodgers
Assistant Director: Jesse Del Fierro
Stage Manager: Donna Sharpe
Dramaturg: Evan Medd
Production Design: Alia Shabab
Poster Design: Sam Mendoza
Light Design: Ajay Badoni
Sound Design: Chris Austman
Costume Design: Jordan Wieben

The play was developed in a production by In Arms Theatre Collective as part of the Edmonton International Fringe Theatre Festival in 2019 with the following cast and creative team:

Yara: Navtej Sandhu
Mona: Liana Bdéwi
Zidan / Fifi: Maher Sinno
Rami / Naseeb: Makram Ayache

Director: Desirée Leverenz
Stage Manager: Roxanne Côté
Production Design: Sofia Lukie
Sound Design: Chris Pereira

SETTING

Beirut, Lebanon.

TIME

Beyond space and time.
1978.
2018.

CHARACTERS

Mona: female, twenty-four years old, light, sprite-like energy.
Yara: female, twenty-four years old, grounded, tree-like energy.
Naseeb: male, twenty-one years old, frantic, ifrit-like energy.
Rami: male, twenty-six years old, fiery, electric-like energy.
Zidan: male, thirty-one years old, level, wolf-like energy. / Fifi: Zidan's
drag persona, phoenix-like energy.
Naseeb and Rami should be played by the same actor.

PUNCTUATION AND TEXT DETAILS

(. . .) Ellipses are used to indicate a lingering, a beat or two, after the line.

(—) Em dashes are used when the line that follows comes in suddenly after, or when the character is frantic in thought.

(/) Forward slashes are used when the line is interrupted by the following line.

[ ] Square brackets are used to show the English translation of Arabic words.

At times, the text will not follow proper grammatical structure, in these cases, the actors are invited to respond to it by playing with tone, inflection, and style. For example: "waitwaitwait" or "we have allah-jesus-shiva-buddha, whoever you like."

PROLOGUE

Beyond space and time.

MONA and YARA enter.

They are walking through memories—their words transforming the stage, glowing into infinity.

MONA: The Green Line.

خطّ التّماس.

YARA: The Green Line is a line of demarcation in a state of war.

خطّ التّماس هو خطّ فاصل بقلب ساحة حرب.

MONA: Imaginary, drawn by a grant designer who cleaves the land with his titanic axe—

خيالي؛ رسمه مصمّم عظيم وشقّ الأرض بفأسه المَهول—

YARA: —separating the conflicting factions. In our civil war, it split our single body into two.

—وفرّق الفرق المتخاصمة. بالحرب الأهليّة، انشقّت البلاد نصّين.

MONA: East Beirut—

بيروت الغربيّة—

YARA: —and West Beirut—

وبيروت الشرقيّة—

MONA & YARA: Christian and Muslim Beirut.

بيروت المسلمة وبيروت المسيحيّة.

YARA: Marked by a no man's land, destroyed by tanks, gunfire, and bombings—

فصل بين أرضين مْشَوْهِتها الدبابات والقنابل والرّصاص خط مش مسمّى—

MONA: —like a stitch across our face.

متل ندبة بنصّ الوجه—

YARA: But the thing about this line is that it was no longer imaginary. The war went on for so long that the natural vegetation began to break through the red stone and a literal green line ran from the southernmost tip of the city and extended into the lip of the Mediterranean Sea.

بس اللّي بميّز هالخطّ بالذات هو إنو ما عاد خيالي. الحرب طوّلت لدرجة إنو النّبات شقّ الحجر الأحمر وبالفعل خطّ أخضر مشي من أقصى جنوب المدينة ووصل لتمّ البحر الأبيض المتوسّط.

MONA: It might have been beautiful—

كان ممكن يكون حلو—

YARA: —if it wasn't so ugly.

—لو ما كان كتير بشع.

MONA: Returned to her nature, these ancient lands gave birth to ancient creatures. Jinns and faeries—

—بس رجعت لطبيعتها، هالأراضي العتيقة ولّدت كائنات قديمة. جنّ وحوريات—

YARA: —shaytans and demons—

—شياطين وووحوش—

MONA: —who roamed in the celestial canopies that no human dared to enter.

—تجوّلوا وكزدروا بفضا الزّيح مطرح ما ما حدا تْجَرَّأ يدعس.

YARA: Even if one wanted to, they would have been shot by the snipers defending their respective territory.

ولو حدا تْجَرَّأ وفات، كانت صابِتُه رصاصة قنّاص عم بِدافع عن ميلته من الأرض.

MONA: But what if a person did get in? What would they find?

ولو قدر حدا يفوت؟ شو كان صار؟

YARA: Who would they find?

مين كان لاقى؟

The stage erupts into a club scene—the hidden queer nightlife of Beirut.

YARA and MONA exit as FIFI enters.

SCENE ONE
A PHOENIX DANCES

2018.

Nightclub.

ZIDAN enters as FIFI, his alter-ego drag persona. FIFI performs her drag number. She flies into the nightclub, her wings ablaze, she is made of fire. She is like a forest fire, consuming the flora, making way for new growth. Her song is infectious. When she finally lands, she stands as tall and regal as the celestial bird she embodies—the phoenix.

RAMI is watching from the audience. As soon as the performance is over, RAMI heads for the exit.

FIFI: La wein reyeh, habibi? *[Where are you going, baby?]*

لوين رايح حبيبي؟

RAMI: Sorry, I don't speak Arabic.

FIFI: Oooh, she doesn't speak Arabic. A foreigner.

RAMI: Hah—I gotta go.

FIFI: The night's just starting—

RAMI: I'm just on my way out.

FIFI: You don't like my show?

RAMI: *(flustered)* Oh god—

FIFI: Which god, habibi? We have allah-jesus-shiva-buddha, whoever you like.

RAMI: All of them.

FIFI: You're very cute.

RAMI: Look, sorry, I have to go. Here.

RAMI extends a dollar to FIFI.

FIFI: Please, honey, I'm not that cheap.

RAMI: I'm so sorry!

FIFI: Is this your first gay bar?

RAMI: No, it's not.

FIFI: I've never seen you around here.

RAMI: It's my first time in Beirut. I really gotta go.

FIFI: That's the smoking exit, baby!

RAMI heads for another exit.

FIFI catches him.

FIFI: I tell you what, you have this cigarette with me, and I'll let you off for thinking I was only worth a dollar.

RAMI: I don't smoke.

FIFI: You'll pick it up; everyone smokes here.

RAMI: I'm okay.

FIFI: I'm Fifi, the Phoenix.

> *RAMI pauses.*

RAMI: The Phoenix?

FIFI: Can't you tell?

> *FIFI extends her hand, much like a queen to her subjects. RAMI shakes it awkwardly.*

RAMI: I'm Rami.

FIFI: What brings you out here tonight?

RAMI: Google.

FIFI: What'd you search, "Hey Google! Where's the closest place I could get some dick?"—

RAMI: Hey, no, come on, that's not why I'm here—

FIFI: Please, honey, look around, that's why we're all here.

RAMI: Sorry to disappoint.

FIFI: We get it, we get it, you're celibate.

RAMI: I'm not—it's just not that kind of night—

FIFI: What kind of night is it?

RAMI: Don't worry about it.

FIFI: Aren't you mysterious?

RAMI: You're the one with the caked-on face—what're you hiding?

FIFI: Nothing at all, baby. Fifi tells it exactly as it is. And right now, she wants to buy you a drink.

RAMI: I really shouldn't drink tonight.

FIFI: Let me get this straight: you come to a gay bar to sit in a corner, not drink, and not fuck. Are you here to kill us?

RAMI: No—no! My god—no!

FIFI: Calm down, sweetie, I'm kidding.

RAMI: It's a weird night.

FIFI: Foreigner, you are mysterious . . . come on . . . one teeny tiny itty bitty drink?

 Beat.

RAMI: All right, Fifi . . . I'll have *a* drink. *One* drink.

FIFI: Amazing. Wait right here. Two of the *BEST* vodka sodas with a twist of lime for our foreigner friend coming right up!

 FIFI exits.

 MONA enters. She takes RAMI in from afar.

 Shift.

 1978.

RAMI is now playing NASEEB. *He stumbles into his apartment late at night.*

MONA: Naseeb.

نسيب؟

NASEEB: Huh?

نعم؟

MONA: Have you been drinking?

كنت عم تشرب؟

NASEEB: What?

شو؟

MONA: Have you been drinking?

كاين عم تشرب؟

NASEEB: Go to bed, Mona.

فوتي نامي منى.

MONA: Where were you?

وين كنت؟

NASEEB: At Ammo Tarik's.

عند عمو طارق.

MONA: I fucking hate that guy!

كس أخت شكله لطارق!

NASEEB: Hey, watch your language!

اتهذّبي.

MONA: Please, *please*, promise me you're not drinking and driving home.

بليز. بليز قلي إنك ما عم تشرب وتسوق.

NASEEB: I'm going to bed.

أنا فايت نام.

MONA: Did you hear what I said?

سمعتني شو قلت؟

NASEEB: I thought you were asleep. It's not a big deal.

فكرِتك نمِتِ. ما تعتلي همّ.

MONA: Naseeb!

نسيب!

NASEEB: It's not. A big. Deal. Okay?

ما. تعتلي. همّ. أوكي؟

NASEEB exits.

SCENE TWO
UNLIKELY FRIENDSHIP

Beyond space and time.

YARA enters.

YARA: I remember that furtive glance as I was packing away my books—

بتذكّر كيف أجت عيني بعينها سرقة أنا وعم ضب كتبي—

MONA: —you looked at me for a hundred thousand years and just as I began to taste your fragrance—

—تأمّلتي فيّي شي مية ألف سنة وشي سرحت بريحتك—

YARA: —I vacuumed the air with a quick clearing of my throat—

—سعلت سعلة صغيرة وانكسر الصّمت—

MONA: —I'm imagining your lips—

—عم بتخايل شفافك—

YARA: —stop it—

—خلص—

MONA: —we both know—

—اتنيناتنا منعرف—

YARA: —we can't let this grow—

—إنو ما فينا نخلّي هالشي يكبر—

MONA: —it won't end well—

—ما حيخلص منيح—

YARA: —not well at all—

—ما حيخلص منيح أبدًا—

MONA: —look at me—

—اتطلّعي فيّي—

YARA: —look away—

—ما تطلّعي فيّي—

MONA: —I keep falling—

—عم بغرق—

YARA: —stop it—

—خلص—

MONA: —you stop—

—إنتي خلص—

YARA: —I don't want this—

—ما بدّي هالشّي—

MONA: —me neither—

—ولا أنا—

YARA: —then look away—

—لكان ما تطلّعي فيّي—

MONA: —I can't.

—ما فيّي.

YARA: I can't.

ما فيّي.

YARA & MONA: —I can't do this—

—ما بقا فيّي—

A moment that turns infinite.

MONA: How long have we been here?

قدّي إلنا هون؟

YARA: For a hundred thousand years.

شي مية ألف سنة.

Shift.

MONA: I didn't look at her for that long. That was meaningless. I was just appreciating her beauty. That's all.

ما تطلّعت فيها هلقد. وَلَوْ. كنت بس عم بتأمّل جمالها. هَيْ هِيِّي. مش أكتر.

YARA: When I was a little girl, Mama shrieked to my aunt, "They found two lasagnas in a car up the street!"

بذكر لما كنت صغيرة إمي عم تعيّط لخالتي وتقلها: «لقوا تنين لازانيا بسيارة عراس الشارع.»

MONA: I like her hair; I might do it like that.

حلو شعرها. بركي بعمل متلها.

YARA: She meant "lesbians."

كان قصدها «لزبيان.»

MONA: That's all, right?

هَيْ هِيِّي. مش أكتر صح؟

YARA: They found two lesbians up the street.

لقوا اتنين لزبيان عراس الشارع.

MONA: I like her shirt.

حلوة قميصتها.

YARA: What's a lesbian, Mama?

شو يعني لزبيان ماما؟

MONA: I like her chest.

حلو صدرها.

YARA: A lesbian is a sick woman who lies with other women.

لزبيان يعني مرا بتنام مع مرا. مريضة يعني.

MONA: I like her breasts.

حلوين ثديَيْها.

YARA: I wanted to say, "Mama, I learn more from your gossip than I do from the books at school"—

كان بدّي قلها «ماما بتعلّم من جَقّاتك أكتر من ما بتعلّم بالمدرسة»—

MONA: —be quiet!—

—اسكتي!—

YARA: —but I stay quiet.

—بس ببقى ساكتة.

Shift.

1978.

The sound of a school bell.

YARA is reading and smoking a cigarette.

MONA: Excuse me, I'm sorry to bother you—

سوري، ما قصدي أزعجك—

YARA looks up from her book.

May I borrow a cigarette?

فيّي استعير سيجارة؟

YARA: You can even keep it.

فيكي تاخديها كمان.

YARA fishes her backpack for her pack of cigarettes. MONA *watches intently.*

YARA hands MONA *the cigarette.*

MONA: Thank you.

مرسي.

YARA: Of course.

يا هلا.

YARA returns to her book.

MONA: Do you have a lighter?

عندك قدّاحة؟

YARA: Sure.

أكيد.

YARA lights the cigarette.

MONA: Thanks—again.

مرسي—بعد مرة.

YARA: *(somewhat irritated, somewhat intrigued)* Of course. Anything else?

يا هلا. شي تاني؟

MONA: You're in Mounir's morning class, right?

إنتي بصفّ منير الصّبح صح؟

YARA: *(holds up the book)* The History of Structural Integrity.

تاريخ السّلامة الهيكليّة.

MONA: Could it be any more boring?

معقول شو بزهِّق؟

YARA: I find it pretty fascinating.

أنا بلاقيه بِسلّي.

MONA: —I was just about to say that.

—كنت حقول نفس الشي.

YARA: Were you now?

ما هيك؟

MONA: No. I really hate that class.

لا. عنجد بكره هالصّف.

They laugh.

YARA: Beautiful necklace.

عقدك حلو.

MONA: Thank you.

مرسي.

YARA: Is it real gold?

دهب؟

MONA: Yeah, Mama gave it to me. It's been in my family for generations—old money—as they say!

إيه من ماما. إلو بْعَيْلِتْنا أجيال—مال قديم—متل ما بقولوا.

YARA: Who has old money these days?

مين بعد عندو مال قديم هالإيّام؟

MONA: I don't know! Maybe I made that up! I'll have to look into it. Hah.

ما بعرف يمكن هي أنا اخترعتها. بدي إسألّك. هه.

YARA: You're peculiar.

فيكي شي . . . غير إنتي.

Beat.

They smoke in silence for a moment.

I'd be careful wearing gold around here. Things aren't what they used
to be.

انتبهي ما بْيِنْلَبَسْ دهب وين ما كان. الإشيا ما عادت متل ما كانت.

MONA puts her hand to her necklace.

MONA: Well this is the only thing that's keeping me protected.

يعني . . . هيدا الشّي الوحيد اللّي حاميني هلق.

YARA: Then it'd be a shame to lose it.

لكان مش حرزانة تْضَيْعيه.

MONA: Look at it.

شوفيه.

MONA holds it up.

YARA: What is it?

شو هيدا؟

MONA: A phoenix.

طير الفينيق.

YARA: That'll keep you protected?

هيدا حَيِحْميكي؟

MONA: Of course! A phoenix has an endless chain of lives braiding into lives. It turns to ash with one breath and comes blazing back to life with the next.

أكيد! طير الفينيق عندو كذا ألف حياة بقلب حياة. بِنَفَسْ بِصير رماد وبِنَفَسْ بْيِخْلَق من جديد.

A phoenix is a promise of eternity.

الفينيق وعد الأزليّة.

YARA: Is that another thing "they" say?

هيك بِقولوا كمان؟

MONA: No, I definitely made that one up. But it deserves a story; it's the only gold we have left in our family. So I'm hoping I find a tall, rich man who can take me far, far away from here.

لا هَيْ عالأكيد أنا اخترعتا. بس بْيِطْلَعْلُه قصّة. هَيْ آخر قطعة دهب بقِيت بالعيلة. فعَمْ بتأمّل لاقيلي شي شبّ طويل وغني ياخدني بعيد من هون.

YARA: You think a man will give you that?

قولك شبّ حيقدملك هالشّي؟

MONA: Well . . . a tall rich one might.

يعني . . . يِمكن إذا كان طويل وغني.

YARA: Good luck with that. For the rest of us without "old money"— we're happy to stay put.

موفَّقة. اللّي متلنا ما عندو مال قديم باقْيين مطرحنا ومبسوطين.

MONA: Oh come on, I see you've got a pretty ring there!

طَوْلي بالك. مبيّن لابسة مَحْبَسْ.

YARA *holds up her fingers. A wedding ring.*

YARA: New money.

مال جديد.

MONA: You're married?

مجوّزة؟

YARA: In a few months.

بعد كَمْ شهر.

MONA: That's exciting!

خَيْ. حلو!

YARA: Thank you.

مرسي.

A moment. They fully see each other.

YARA *looks away.*

MONA *stays.*

I—I gotta go.

لازم—روح.

YARA *begins to exit.*

MONA: What's your name?

شو إسمك؟

YARA: Yara.

يارا.

MONA: I'm Mona.

أنا منى.

YARA: Nice to meet you.

اتشرّفنا.

They exit.

SCENE THREE
THE BACKROOM

Beyond space and time.

NASEEB enters.

He is in the entanglement of the Green Line. Vines encircle vines and rocky parts of the earth are suspended in the air. Ultraviolet green and purple lights twinkle through the veins of the flora surrounding him, the veils of the world thinning. He is lodged in between our world and the next.

He looks at the spirits sitting in front of him.

NASEEB: I always hoped I would become a bird after I died.

كنت دايمًا إتأمّل صير طير بس يِجي الوقت.

Death seems to always come in the fall of night and I asked my family to bring my body back here . . . Lebanon. Her mountains cradle around the sea like my mother used to hold me when I was a little boy. I thought I might be free to fly into the heavens. But instead, here I am on the Green Line. Suspended.

كأنّو الموت دايمًا بيجي بالليّل وأنا طلبت من عيلتي يجيبوني لهون. علبنان. جباله بيحضنوا البحر متل ما أمّي كانت تغمرني لما كنت صغير. فكّرت حكون حرّ وطير بين السّماوات. قمت لقيتْ حالي عخطّ التّماس. معلّق.

I heard you speak at my funeral, Rami. I heard you when you said my name: Naseeb Aswad Al'asfour, 1957 to 2018, beloved husband and father. I heard Sureh al Yasin chant through the funeral hall. I saw your tears and your mother's tears wash over my body.

سْمعتَك عم تحكي بجنازتي رامي. سْمعتَك عم تقول إسمي: نسيب أسود العصفور، ١٩٧٥-٢٠١٨، زوج وأب محبّ. سمعت سورة الياسين من قلب الحيطان. شفت دموعك ودموع أمك عم يغسلوني.

I'm with you, Rami. And as they lower my body into the ground, I remember that the earth has secrets if you're willing to look for them. This soil turns my body into a spirit and the memories I thought I long escaped are returning.

أنا معك رامي. وهنّي وعم بِنزلوني بالأرض، بتذكّر إنو الأرض في بقلبها أسرار وإنّك قادر تلاقيهن إذا كنت مستعدّ تْدَوِّر عليهن. هيدا التراب عم بِحَوِّل جسمي لروح والذّكريات اللّي فكّرت حالي هربت منهن عم يرجعوا.

But I've asked you to do for me one final task . . . instead, you're drinking and dancing. On the night of my funeral.

بس طلبت منك خدمة أخيرة . . . وأنت قاعد عم تشرب وترقص. ليلة دفني.

Do you see me? *Can* you see me?

شايفني؟ قادر تشوفني؟

Rami? Rami?

رامي؟ رامي؟

Shift.

ZIDAN enters.

2018.

The club music pounding dimly in the near distance. FIFI *has brought* RAMI *to the backroom of the club.*

FIFI: Welcome to the backroom, Rami.

RAMI: You're not gonna tell me this is where all the magic happens, are you?

FIFI: Please, baby, I'm not that tacky.

RAMI: Aw too bad, I was hoping you were.

FIFI: Okay lemme take a guess: not out to Mom and Dad, got in a fight with your homophobic uncle, looked up the closest gay bar, badabing badaboom, here you are!

RAMI: Who says I'm not out?

FIFI: Ooh, the plot thickens.

RAMI: Keep guessing, I'm really starting to enjoy this.

FIFI: *(playfully)* Just as I'm really starting to get bored of it.

RAMI: How about for each hint I give you, you clean off a part of your face?

FIFI: You're cute, wallah, but if you're telling me this makeup is not clean, you have to leave right (now)—

RAMI: —I'm saying I want to see the real you—

FIFI: —Habibti, this is the real me.

RAMI: No, no, the real you has beautiful eyes.

FIFI: Okay . . .

> *RAMI begins to play with FIFI's hair. FIFI is enjoying it.*

RAMI: Beautiful hair.

FIFI: Mhmm . . .

RAMI: A beautiful beard.

FIFI: But not beautiful contouring?

RAMI: I was just about to say that!

FIFI: Mhmm . . . I thought you weren't looking for sex tonight.

RAMI: You're the one who got me these drinks!

FIFI: I didn't realize it'd make you a hummus-hunting thirst trap.

> *RAMI stops playing with FIFI's hair. He's embarrassed.*

RAMI: Okay-okay-okay-okay, Fifi, I'm confused because you are the sexiest drag queen I've ever met—

FIFI: It's a good thing most drag queens are gay guys.

RAMI: Not all of them!

FIFI: You are so progressive. Are you from Amsterdam?

RAMI: Canada.

FIFI: How cute.

RAMI: So are you.

FIFI: From Canada? No, habibti, I was born and raised here.

RAMI: I meant cute too.

FIFI: You're really hoping to see me without makeup, aren't you?

RAMI: A little bit. Aren't you afraid, dressed like that?

FIFI: Aren't you afraid to wear turtlenecks?

> *RAMI laughs.*

RAMI: They're in style!

FIFI: What's there to be afraid of? That crowd was eating it up.

RAMI: But what about past these walls?

FIFI: What do you know about past these walls?

RAMI: Honestly, not a whole lot. But for a place so full of war, it's surprisingly fun.

FIFI: Excuse me?

RAMI: What? Oh no that's not what I meant—

FIFI: You come here, party, eat, sleep, shit everywhere, then leave. I'm sure it is surprisingly fun.

RAMI: I'm not here to party.

FIFI: That's what they all say—pass me the wipes.

> *RAMI hands FIFI some makeup wipes. FIFI methodically removes her makeup.*

I'm gonna take my face off now. Not for you—but because I need to get home—

RAMI: So you are afraid!—

FIFI: No—I just know this city better than you do, Foreigner—

RAMI: My name is Rami—

FIFI: I've decided it's Foreigner.

Beat.

RAMI: What's your name?

FIFI: Fifi, I already said.

RAMI: What's your real name.

FIFI: Mmm . . . Now we both have our secrets.

RAMI: Wow, you are a handful, aren't you?

FIFI: Baby, I've been a handful since I came into this world. My mother swears I was born singing and dancing and haven't really stopped much since.

RAMI: Has she seen you perform?

FIFI: Are you crazy? No. My parents put me in all the right places: Boy Scouts, an all-boys Catholic school, would you believe that I was even the youth leader of my church group for a while? All the things a straight little man should do.

RAMI: No way—

FIFI: Oh yes, Baba would even take me bird hunting in the mountains.

RAMI: So manly of you, Fifi.

FIFI: I know. But when I finally killed my first bird, I cried like a little faggot and that sealed the deal for him. I didn't want to do it, but he kept patting me on the shoulder, encouraging me at first. But at some point, it started to feel like a threat. And when I killed it, he was hysterical. "Ibnee el batal!" "My son is a hero!"

But I froze.

I stood there watching the bird plummet from the sky like a bullet in slow motion, snow up to my ankles, the frozen trees silently judging my massacre. And then I began to cry, this faggy little son, weeping for a bird that was going to be our dinner.

He slapped me so hard I fell into the snow.

> *Beat.*

Am I afraid to dress like this? I've seen it all, baby. Harassed, bullied, threatened, even arrested for a night. I simply don't give a fuck anymore.

> *FIFI approaches RAMI . . . a little unpredictably.*

Can you zip me down?

RAMI: Uh . . . sure.

> *RAMI unzips FIFI's dress.*

> *FIFI heads to the exit for privacy.*

Oh, she's modest!

FIFI: Can't give it all away, baby.

> *FIFI exits.*

> *RAMI picks up another glass of alcohol and takes a drink.*

> *He pulls a photograph out of his pocket. He looks at it carefully. Then he puts it away. The sounds of a small clash, firing of guns.*

MONA enters.

1978.

MONA: Naseeb! Come in, come in!

نسيب! فوت لجوّا! فوت!

Shift.

SCENE FOUR
THE NEIGHBOURHOOD

1978.

The apartment.

MONA: Come inside, quickly!

فوت بسرعة!

NASEEB rushes into the apartment.

Are you okay? I heard shooting. What are you doing out there?

صارلك شي؟ سمعت قواص. شو عم تعمل عندك؟

NASEEB: It was up the street—I'm okay—

القواص عراس الشارع—أنا منيح، ما بِني شي—

MONA: Why are you out there this late in the evening?

شو عم تعمل برّا بآخر هاللّيل؟

NASEEB: Mona, settle down.

منى. روقي.

MONA: Sit down, please, I'll get you some water. Naseeb, this is the fourth time I'm hearing clashes in our area this week! People are getting reckless. Don't get involved with them!

اقعد شوي بليز. حَجِبلك كبّاية مي. نسيب، هي رابع مرة هالأسبوع بسمع اشتباكات وقواص عنا بالحي! النّاس صايرة بلا مخ. ما تفوت معهن!

NASEEB: You want me to stay home all day?

شو بدَّك ياني إبقى بالبيت كل النهار؟

MONA: Yes! Exactly, habibi!

إيه! بالظبط حبيبي!

NASEEB is peering out the window.

NASEEB: Mona—

منى—

MONA: —Here, sit sit sit, please relax, ya albi.

تعا—اقعد اقعد اقعد، بليز روق يا قلبي.

She sits him down.

Just let your big sister take care of you. I made you some knaffeh. I just warmed it up in the oven. I'll be right back.

خلّي أختك الكبيرة تهتم فيك، عْمِلْتِلّك كنافة. سخّنتها بالفرن. يلا دقيقة لجيبها.

NASEEB: Mona, wait—

منى انطري—

MONA: No more talking. I want you to stay put—

بزيادة حكي، بدي ياك تضلّ عندك—

NASEEB: But—

بس—

MONA: Here.

هَيْ.

MONA flicks on the radio.

Listen, relax, listen to the song.

اسمع، روق، اتسمّع عهالغنية.

NASEEB: Mona, Ammo Tarik and I have been talking to a lawyer from Sin El Fil.

منى، أنا وعمو طارق عم نحكي مع محامي من سنّ الفيل.

Beat.

MONA: Why are you going across the line?

ليه عم تِقْطَع الخطّ؟

NASEEB: It's nothing to get our hopes up about, but there might be a way for us to get out of here.

بعد ما في شي نتأمّل فيه، بس يمكن يكون في طريقة نطلع فيها من هون.

MONA: What do you think I'm doing at the university? Let me finish my education, then we can leave.

شو مفكّرني قاعدة عم بعمل بالجامعة؟ خلّيني خلص شهادتي ومنفلّ.

She exits to grab the knaffeh.

NASEEB: The lawyers say they got the files back from the raids. Some of Mama and Baba's missing documents might be in there.

المحامين عم بِقولوا قِدروا يستحصلوا عجزء من الملفّات بعد الغارات. يمكن وراق ماما وبابا النّاقصين بيناتهن.

She returns with the food.

MONA: Khalas, kol kol *[enough, eat eat]*, enough talking. I don't want to hear about this right now.

خلص، كول، كول. بكفّي حكي. ما بدي إحكي بهالموضوع هلق.

NASEEB eats the spoonful she's thrusting his way.

NASEEB: God, this is amazing.

يْسلّم إيديكِ! كتير طيبة!

MONA: Sahtein, habibi. [*Bon appétit, my dear.*]

صحتين حبيبي.

He takes the plate and continues to eat.

NASEEB: You make it just like Mama.

بْتِطْلَع معك متل ماما.

MONA: What would you do without me?

قلّي شو بتعمل إذا بِصرلي شي؟

NASEEB: La sama'allah. [*God forbid.*]

لا سمح الله.

He continues eating.

All I'm saying is that Baba might have a property in the old town—
Ammo Tarik knows the ins and outs; he took care of Baba's company's
paperwork for years—

كل اللّي عم قوله إنو يمكن بابا يكون عنده شقفة أرض بالضيعة—وعمو طارق عندو كلّ المعلومات
بيعرف الشّاردة والواردة، هو اهتمّ بوراق شركة بابا عسنين—

MONA: Ammo Tarik is also a creep who's wanted to marry me since I
was born.

عمّو طارق كمان زلمة غريب الأطوار كان بدّو يتجوّزني من أوّل ما خلقت.

NASEEB: It's not about that.

مش هي القصّة هلق.

MONA: It's always about that with that man. Look, Naseeb, my
professor thinks I'd be a strong candidate for an international
internship program.

هي دايما القصّة مع هالزّلمة. اسمع نسيب، أستاذي بالجامعة عم بِقلّي إنو عندي فرصة ينقّوني لروح
أعمل دورة تدريبيّة برا.

NASEEB: Mona—

منى—

MONA: *That's* our way to get out of here—

بِهَيْ الطّريقة مْنطلع من هون—

NASEEB: And where do you even want to go?

لَوين مفكرة تروحي أصلًا؟

MONA: France? Norway? Maybe Canada. Who knows?

فرنسا؟ النّرويج؟ يمكن كندا. مين بيعرف؟

NASEEB: And you'll leave me all alone here?

وحَتتركيني هون وحدي؟

MONA: You'll be another woman's problem by then.

حَتكون مشكلة مرا غيري بوقتها.

NASEEB: Lucky her!

إيه نيّالها!

MONA: In the meantime—I think I found you a job. I've been speaking with Mr. Said. He said he could use someone to man the store for him in the evenings. It's close to the apartment and it's a modest income. I told him you might be interested in doing that.

وبهالوقت—بعتقد لْقيتلَك شغل. كنت عم بِحكي مع أستاذ سعيد. قال عايِز حدا يساعده بالمحلّ المَسويّات. المحلّ قريب عالبيت والمدخول ما بو شي، قلتلّو بِهمّك الموضوع.

NASEEB: What?

شو؟

MONA: It'll give you something good to do with your time.

بِتْعَبّي وقتك بشي مفيد.

NASEEB: I'm busy with these documents right now—

مشغول بالوراق هلق—

MONA: I know, habib—

بعرف حبيب—

NASEEB: No, Mona, please don't go around talking to Mr. Said or anyone else. People will start talking about me. Is that what you want?

لا مني، بليز ما تروحي تحكي أستاذ سعيد أو أي حدا تاني من ورا ضهري. بكرا بِتبلِّش العالم تحكي. هيدا اللّي بدك ياه؟

MONA: I'm just trying to help you.

عم جرّب ساعدك.

NASEEB: Well stop!

إيه وقفي عندك!

MONA: Haram le mne' ma'ak [*It's a shame to be good to you.*]

حرام المنيح معك أنت.

She heads for the exit.

NASEEB: Hey, wait—Mona—wait . . . I know heyete—things are not easy since we lost them. But I think if I can get these documents, it's going to change things for the best. Ammo Tarik is really trying to help us.

لحظة، مني—انطري—بعرف حياتي . . . الإشيا ما عادت سهلة من وقت ما خسرناهن. بس بعتقد رح يتحسّن وضعنا بس جيب هالوراق. عمّو طارق عم بِجرِّب يساعدنا.

MONA: So am I.

وأنا كمان.

She exits.

Shift.

NASEEB moves across the stage, becoming RAMI.

2018.

The backroom of the club.

ZIDAN enters.

ZIDAN: My name is Zidan.

RAMI: Zidan. Wow.

ZIDAN: I'm going to kiss you now.

RAMI: That would be nice.

They kiss.

ZIDAN: Beautiful necklace.

RAMI abruptly tucks it away.

RAMI: Uh thanks—I never really wear this out.

ZIDAN: Why not? It's stunning and is delicious with your eyes.

RAMI: It's complicated.

ZIDAN: You stole it?

RAMI: Something like that.

ZIDAN: Suspicious liar boy comes to nightclub with stolen gold necklace hanging from his neck, *doesn't* want to kill everyone. Very mysterious.

RAMI laughs.

RAMI: Oh shut up.

ZIDAN: I'll figure you out, Rami.

Follow me for the VIP life, baby—

RAMI: Okay—

They exit.

SCENE FIVE
ASSIGNMENTS

Beyond space and time.

Memories glow in the air.

MONA and YARA enter.

MONA: When I was a little girl, Baba would take me to the highest of his cranes and give me a view of the entire city. It looked so different back then.

لـمّا كنت صغيرة بابا كان يْطلِّعني على أعلى رافعة ويْفرجيني المدينة من فوق. كان شكلها كتير غير.

YARA: I was born in a tent.

أنا خْلقت بخيمة.

MONA: He would point out all the buildings that he helped build. He was a foreman—one of the best in Beirut. He would always tell me if I could build buildings, I could do anything.

كان يْدِلْني عالبنايات اللّي ساعد بتعميرهن. كان معلّم الملعمين، من الأشطر ببيروت. كان دايمًا يقلّي إذا بقدر عَمِّر بنايات، فيّي أعمل أيّ شي.

YARA: Bloodied walls, graffiti monsters, and bullet shells were the playgrounds of my childhood.

حيطان مرشوشة دم، وحوش غرافيتي، ورصاصات فاضية . . . كنّا نلعب بيناتن.

MONA: From that high up, I truly thought we were flying.

من فوق، كنت حسّ كأنوا عنجد طايرين.

YARA: And Mama is a warrior woman.

وإمّي مرا مناضلة.

MONA: I kept imagining if I jumped out of the crane, wings would peel off my back, like an angel.

كنت ضلّ أتخايل إنو إذا بنطّ عن الرافعة، حَيِطْلَعْلي جوانح متل الملايكة.

YARA: She ate cigarettes for breakfast and even the men in our alleys would cower at her sight.

كانت تنفّخ سيجارة عالتّرويقة. وكانوا رجال الحي يزمّوا بس يشوفوها.

MONA: At first, I would glide over the city. Then, with each flap, I go higher and higher and even higher.

أوّل شي بَعِمْلو، بْطوف فوق المدينة، بعدين مع كلّ ضربة جناح بِطلع أكتر وبْعلّي أكتر.

YARA: I remember a fig tree at the edge of our camp. Every day, Baba plucked a fruit and sliced it into perfect thirds: one for Mama, one for me, and one for him.

بتذكّر كان في شجرة تين عَطَرَف المخيّم عنا. كان بابا كل يوم يقطف منها تينة ويقطّعها ٣ أتلات: تلت لماما، تلت لإلي وتلت لإلو.

MONA: The earth becomes so small until I can't see it.

الأرض بْتِصغَر لحدّ ما تبطّل مْبَيْنة.

YARA: One day I asked him, "Baba, why don't you just pluck three figs?"
He said, "We don't ask for more than what the world can give us."
"But there are so many fruits on that tree."
"Just as well, there are so many people in our camp. There are others we are responsible to."

في نهار سألتُه «بابا، ليه ما بْتُقطُف ٣ تينات؟»
قال لي، «ما مُنطلب أكتر من ما الحياة بتعطينا.»
«بس في كتير تين بالشّجرة.»
«وفي كتير ناس بالمخيّم. في غيرنا.»

MONA: And the earth vanishes into a mote of dust.

والأرض بتختفي كأنها نقطة غبرة.

YARA: After the war began, Baba was killed, and we were forced to resettle with the other Muslims in the west of the city.

بعد ما بلّشت الحرب، انقتل بابا، وانجبرنا نقعد مع المسلمين الباقيين بغرب المدينة.

MONA: But I can only see the Green Line. No matter how high I fly, I could still see the Green Line.

بس فيّي شوف خطّ التّماس. قد ما عْليت، بضلّ بشوف خطّ التّماس.

YARA: And Mama used what she could of her money to put me in university. I went to study engineering.

وماما استعملت اللّي بقي معها من المصاري لتْحُطني بالجامعة. درست هندسة.

MONA: I keep trying to escape the Green Line—

عم ضلّ جرّب أهرب من خطّ التّماس—

YARA: —studying to escape this war—

—أدرس لأهرب من الحرب—

MONA: —by studying—

—بالدّرس—

YARA: —like a stitch across our face—

—متل ندبة معلّمة بنصّ الوجه—

MONA: —Baba always said, "Your brother will never succeed in school, so it's up to you to do well and get you both out of here."

—بابا كان دايمًا يقول «خيِّك ما حَيِفْلَح بالعلم، فعليكي إنتي إنو تنجحي واتْطلعيه معك من هون.»

YARA: I don't want a lot. Just to survive. To live, maybe a little better than Mama.

ما بدّي كتير. بدّي بس إنو إنْفُد، ما موت. عيش يمكن شوي أحسن من ماما.

MONA: That's a lot of pressure on a person.

هيدا عبء كبير عالواحد.

YARA: "I believe in God . . . " Mama says, "because he sent me a daughter who has a mind to build us homes."

«بآمن بالله . . . لأنو بَعَتْلي بنت عندها عقل بِعَمِّرِلْنا بيوت.» هيك ماما قالت.

MONA: After Mama and Baba died, I had to complete my studies at all costs—

بعد ما ماتوا ماما وبابا، كان لازم خلّص شهادتي بأيّ طريقة—

YARA: She said, "You will build us all homes."

قالت «حَتْعَمْريلنا بيوت إلنا كلنا.»

MONA: —and then I met her—

—والتقيتْ فيها—

YARA: I stopped believing in anything a long time ago.

وقّفت آمن بأيّ شي من زمان.

MONA: And it's as if I've known her for a hundred thousand years.

وكأنّي بعرفها من مية ألف سنة.

YARA: —and then I met her—

—والتقيتْ فيها—

Beat. YARA *looks at* MONA.

And it's as if I've known her for a hundred thousand years.

وكأنّي بعرفها من مية ألف سنة.

MONA: One cigarette turned to two, turned to three, turned infinity for a chance to speak to her.

سيجارة صارت تْنين، وتلاتة، وأربعة ومية ألف فرصة لإحكي معها.

YARA: We're *only* friends.

نحنا رفقة، بس.

MONA: Only friends.

بس رفقة.

YARA: That's all—

—مش أكتر

MONA: One night we were at my house, working on an assignment.

في نهار كنا عندي بالبيت، عم نِدرُس.

Shift.

YARA *and* MONA *at the apartment.*

1978.

YARA: I think we'll get a better grade if we do Shibam Hadramawt.

بعتقد حنجيب علامة أعلى إذا منشتغل ع شبام حضرموت.

MONA: The buildings in Yemen?

المباني باليمن؟

YARA: Yes, they're ancient skyscrapers made from mud and brick—they're still standing today.

إيه. ناطحات سحاب قديمة معمولة من حجر وطين—وبعدهن واقفين لليوم.

MONA: But no one even knows how the pyramids got to the middle of the desert. I've read it might have been gods or aliens or—

بس ما حدا بيعرف كيف وصلوا الأهرامات عنّص الصحراء. قريت إنو يمكن الآلهة أو كائنات فضائية—

YARA: That's stupid.

بلا هبل.

MONA: You're being rude.

ما تكوني وقحة.

YARA: Let's stick to the facts—

خلّينا نركّز عالوقايع—

MONA: Okay—the pyramids are the largest in the ancient world. If that alone isn't enough reason—

أوكي—الأهرامات هنّي أكبر عمار بالعالم القديم، إذا هيدا لحاله مانّو سبب كافي—

YARA: —the pyramids of Cholula in Mexico are the largest in the ancient world.

—أهرامات الخولولا بالمكسيك هنّي الأكبر بالعالم القديم.

MONA flips through her textbook.

MONA: No, that can't be right.

لا مش مظبوط.

YARA: It is. How much research have you done?

مْبلا. قدي قارية عنهن؟

MONA: Yara!

يارا!

YARA: I'd like for us to get a good grade—

بدي نْجيب علامة منيحة—

MONA: And you think I don't?

شو أنا ما بدّي؟

YARA: I'm a bit more prepared, that's all I'm saying.

أنا مْحَضّرة شوي أكتر، هيدا كلّ اللّي عم قوله.

MONA: If we can't even agree on what structure—

إذا مش قادرين نتّفق عشو—

YARA: —let's do Shibam.

خلّينا نعمل شبام—

MONA: No.

لا.

YARA: Stop acting like a child.

بلا ولدنة.

MONA: Don't speak to me like that!

ما تحكيني هيك!

MONA begins packing her belongings.

YARA: Wait—wait, Mona, stop—

لحظة- لحظة، منى، وقفي—

MONA: No.

لا.

YARA: I'm sorry, hey, sorry.

YARA gently stops MONA.

I'm sorry—

سوري، اسمعيني، بعتذر.

Beat.

MONA: It's just an assignment.

كلّو دوفوار.

YARA: I'm sorry.

بعتذر.

Beat.

What's this about?

شو القصّة؟

MONA: Nothing . . .

ماشي . . .

YARA: *Obviously* something—

واضح إنو في شي—

MONA: No . . . forget it.

لا . . . إنسي.

YARA: —Mona . . .

—منى . . .

Beat.

MONA: Did you ever travel with your family? Before all of this . . . hell. God, I don't even remember what it was like before.

سافرتي شي مرّة مع أهلك؟ قبل كل هال . . . جحيم. أوف. ما بقا بتذكّر كيف كانوا الإشيا قبل هلق.

It's stupid . . . but the pyramids were the only place we travelled together.

سخيفة القصّة بس الأهرامات كانوا المحلّ الوحيد اللّي رحنا عليه مع بعض. كعيلة.

A long pause as MONA *considers what to say next.*

When I was seven, my parents took me and Naseeb to Cairo.

لمّا كان عمري ٧، أهلي أخدونا إلي ولنسيب عمصر.

YARA: Oh, I see.

آه، أوكي.

MONA: Those bricks are enormous, Yara. They're nothing like the pictures. Have you been?

حجر الأهرامات شي ضخم يارا. مش متل الصّور. رحتي شي مرة؟

YARA: No.

لا.

MONA: At first, I was so terrified. But Mama spoke of Allah building these stones by his will, sculpting them from rocks in faraway lands, breathing magic into each and every one of them. She told me if we sat on the rocks, we could feel the breathing of Allah. And so we sat together, breathing, listening, until we saw the sun slip into the horizon.

أوّل شي، كنت مرعوبة. بس ماما قالت إنو هالحجر تْعمّر بإرادة الله، قال هو نَحَتْهُن من صخر أرض بعيدة، ونفخ سحر بكلّ حجر. قالتلي إنو إذا قعدنا عالحجر فينا نحسّ بِنَفَس الله فيهن. فقعدنا مع بعض، عم ناخد نَفَسْ وعم نِتسمّع لحدّ ما تْخبّت الشّمس ورا الأفق.

Then of course, Naseeb starts climbing the pyramid like a fucking idiot and Baba is chasing after him to get him down. Mama and I lost it.

وبعدين أكيد طلع نسيب يْعَرْبِش عالهرم متل الحمار وبابا صار لاحْقُه لَيْنَزّلُه. أنا وماما جَنَّيْنا.

YARA: That's amazing.

شو حلو.

Beat.

No. I've never travelled anywhere like that with my family. I don't know a time before war. It's always been escape.

لا. أنا ما سافرت عمحلّ مع عيلتي هيك. ما بعرف شي قبل الحرب. كنّا دايمًا عم نهرب. من شي.

MONA: I'm sorry.

سوري.

YARA: You don't have to be. That trip sounds beautiful . . . I think we should do the pyramids.

لا ما خصّك. شكلها كانت حلوة هالرّحلة . . . أوكي منشتغل عالأهرامات.

They hold each other's gaze.

NASEEB rushes in with a folder—the documents from the lawyers.

NASEEB: I got them! I got them! I got the papers!

لقيتهن! لقيتهن! لقيت الوراق!

MONA: Naseeb!

نسيب!

NASEEB: I told you I could it!

قلتلِّك!

MONA: Do what?

شو قلتلِّي؟

NASEEB: We thought, for sure, we lost them in the raids—

فكَّرنا إنو ضاعوا بالغارات—

MONA: You went across the line again?

رجعت قطعت الخطّ؟

NASEEB: —but thanks to Ammo Tarik, we got them!

—بس كَتَّر خيره عمّو طارق، لقاهن!

MONA: What are you talking about?

عن شو عم تحكي؟

NASEEB: Mona . . . Mama and Baba left us a plot of land.

منى . . . ماما وبابا تركولنا شقفة أرض.

MONA: What?

نعم؟

NASEEB: In the Chouf.

بالشوف.

Beat.

MONA: That's . . . wonderful.

أوف . . . هَيْ خبريّة.

NASEEB: It doesn't sound like you think it's wonderful.

ما شكلها خبريّة حلوة.

MONA: Naseeb, I told you I need to finish school.

نسيب، قلتلّك لازم خلّص جامعة.

NASEEB: What?

شو؟

MONA: How will I get to class if we're four hours into the mountains?

كيف حَأوصل عالجامعة إذا نحنا بالجبل بعاد أربع ساعات؟

NASEEB: There's a war going on around us.

في حرب مني. نحنا بحرب.

MONA: This is important to me, habibi.

هيدا الشّي كتير مهم إلي حبيبي.

NASEEB: Are you being serious?

عم تحكي جدّ هلق؟

MONA: With my degree, I—we—can leave Lebanon. What're we gonna do up there—camp out on our plot of land?

بس آخد شهادتي، بِصير فيني- بصير فينا نفلّ من لبنان. شو حَنعمل بالجبل؟ نْخَيِّم عشقفة الأرض؟

NASEEB: Ammo Tarik has family—we can stay with them until there's time to build.

عمّو طارق عندو عيلة—فينا نضلّ عندهن لَبِين ما كنا عمرنا.

MONA: How are we gonna afford to build? Habibi, where are we gonna get the money?

وكيف حَنْعمِّر؟ حبيبي من وين بدنا نجيب المصاري؟

NASEEB: I'll work.

حَإشتغل.

MONA: Do you understand how much it costs to build a house?

بْتعرف قدّي بِكلّف تْعمِّر بيت؟

NASEEB: I'll use the money in the inheritance.

باخُد مصاري من الوِرتة.

Beat.

MONA: That's for my studies.

مصاري الورتة لجامعتي.

NASEEB: It's in my name.

الورتة بإسمي.

MONA: No, no, Naseeb, that's for my studies.

لا لا نسيب. الورتة لجامعتي.

NASEEB: Mona . . .

منى . . .

MONA: Naseeb! I'm a few months away from finishing. Then I'll be an engineer! That's our way out of here!

نسيب! رح خلّص بعد كم شهر وبْصير مهندسة! ومْنطلع من هون!

NASEEB: Have you seen the blockades going through the middle of the city? They've split us into two. Have you missed that?! Ammo Tarik said if the Christians—

شِفتي الحواجز بنصّ المدينة؟ قَسَمونا نصّين. لاحظتي؟! عمّو طارق قال إذا المسيحيّي—

MONA: Forget him for a second!

نْسيلي عمّو طارق دقيقة!

NASEEB: He's trying to help us!

عم بِجرِّب يساعدنا!

MONA: Are you fucking serious?

عم تِتْمَنْيَك عليّي؟

NASEEB: Watch your mouth!—

ما تْخَبّصي حَكي!—

MONA: —are you fucking serious, Naseeb?! This is a huge decision; I am allowed to weigh in!

—عم تِحكي من كلّ عقلَك نسيب؟! هيدا قرار مصيري؛ وأنا إلي رأي فيه!

NASEEB: I'm doing what I see best for this family!

كل شي عم بعملو لمصلحة هالعيلة!

MONA: You're not Baba!

مانّك بابا!

NASEEB: *I'M TRYING TO TAKE CARE OF YOU!!!*

عم جرِّب. إهتمّ. فيكي!!!!!!

    Beat.

Of us.

فينا.

I'm trying my best. Just . . . stop being so difficult. Stop it! You don't know what's happening out there. You've got your head so far in your books learning how to build buildings, you don't see them falling all around you. Last night, they destroyed an entire village along the sea. Did you forget what happened to Mama and Baba?

عم جرِّب. عم بَعْمُل كلّ جهدي . . . حاج تْصعبيها عليّي. خلص بقا! مانِك مستوعبة شو عم بِصير برا. راسك غرقان بالكتب لتعمري بنايات ومانك شايفتيهن عم يُقْشطوا حواليكي. مبارح باللّيل نَزَّلوا ضيعة متل ما هيّي عالسّاحل. نسيتي شو صار بماما وبابا؟

MONA: Of course not.

أكيد لا.

NASEEB: Did you?! Because they were just going to a party; they were going to a party and she was wearing her favourite silver dress. Apparently it was too low or too high or I don't know—

نسيتي؟! لأنو كانوا رايحين يسهروا؛ كانوا رايحين عالسّهرة وكانت ماما لابسة فستانها الفضي، أكثر فستان بتحبُّه، وأبصر كان كتير قصير مدري كتير طويل شو بعرّفني—

MONA: Naseeb . . .

نسيب . . .

NASEEB: Because now when you go to a fucking party, it's enough reason to blast you open with an AK-47! We're living like animals, Mona! They didn't even let us see their bodies!

لأنو صار تروحي عسهرة هلق سبب كافي إنو يطخّوكي بالAK٤٧! عايشين متل الحيوانات منى! ما حتى خلّونا نشوفهن!

MONA: Okay . . . okay . . . it's okay . . .

أوكي . . . أوكي . . . روق . . .

NASEEB: I should have done something then—

كان لازم أعمل شي . . . كان لازم . . .

MONA: You couldn't have done anything, habibi . . .

ما كان فيك تعمل شي حبيبي . . .

NASEEB: God, if something happens to you, I can't imagine—I can't—

إذا بِصرلك شي، ما فيّي إتخايل—ما فيّي—

MONA: Naseeb, I'm okay. We're okay. Alhamdullilah. Alhamdullilah. [*Thank God. Thank God.*]

نسيب، أنا منيحة. نحنا مناح. الحمدالله. الحمدالله.

 Long beat.

NASEEB: We're going to the mountains . . .

حَنطلع عالجبل . . .

MONA: Let's sleep on it. Okay? We'll talk tomorrow.

خلّينا نفكّر بالموضوع. أوكي؟ منحكي بكرا.

MONA and NASEEB exit.

SCENE SIX
BUTTERFLY EFFECT

Beyond space and time.

YARA moves through the Green Line, her spirit dissolving into the spirits of the line. Again, memories glow around her.

YARA: If this war takes me, I want to be left out for the birds. I want to be plucked, eyes and limbs by the same creatures that circle the sky. This earth never made much sense to me because I don't think I make much sense to it: first a Palestinian: refugee by birth. Now: thrust into another country's war. I can't imagine being in the sky outside the belly of a bird.

إذا أخدتني هالحرب، بدّي يِنْتَرَك جسمي للعصافير. بدّي الطيور اللّي ساكنة بالسما تُنْقُر عيوني وأطرافي. ما بحياتي فهمتها هالأرض أصلًا وما بحياتها فهمتني. من أوّلها: فلسطينيّة، لاجئة بالولادة. وهلق مزتوتة بحرب بلد تاني. ما قادرة إتخايل حالي بالسّما غير بقلب عصفور.

I am armoured, I am suspicious, and I am angry.

أنا قاسية. قلقانة. غضبانة.

And I'm to be married to Karam in a few months. He is a pious man—a good man. He reminds me of Baba. He doesn't offer too much, but he'll give me quiet. He'll give Mama quiet, and God knows she deserves it.

ورح أتجوّز كرم بعد كم أسبوع. رجّال مؤمن—آدمي. بِذكّرني ببابا. ما بِقدّم كتير بس حَيْجِبْلي راحة البال. وحَيْهَدّي بال ماما. الله بيعلم إنو لازملها.

We've been running for too long. We've only ever known bullets and battered bodies and death has become a necklace I'm all too familiar with.

إلنا زمان عم نهرب. ما عرفنا غير الرّصاص والجثث. والموت صار متل سِنسلة لابستها وتعوّدت عليها.

I first wore this necklace at seven years old when Mama is buying me a sandwich from our favourite shop along the sea. I remember it a beautiful day. Hot, sunny, and the skies are a dusted dry blue—then a man comes in holding a pistol.

أوّل مرة لبست السّنسلة كان عمري ٧ سنين كانت ماما عم تْجِبلي سندويشة من محل كتير منحبو عالبحر. بتذكّر كان نهار حلو. شوب، شمس وسما زرقا مرشوشة غيوم—وبِفوت زلمة مسلّح.

I say, "Mama, what's wrong?" She replies, "Shush, stay quiet." The man fires one, two, three, four, five shots into the body of the store clerk. The cadaver lies, eyes open, staring his crystal green irises into my own. I could have sworn he smiles at me. I begin to cry—Mama cups my mouth—I can't breathe—Mama holds tighter—I think I'm going to die—the man leaves the shop: and I inhale.

بِتْطَلَّع بماما وبقلها «ماما شو في؟» بِتجاوبني «شش. ولا كلمة.» الزلمة بقوِّص ضرب، تنين، تلاتة، أربعة، خمسة بجسم صاحب المحل. بْتوقع جثته، عيونه الخضر مفتْحة، صوب عيوني. كأني شفتُه ضِحكْلي. والله. بْبلِّش إبكي—ماما بِتْغطّيلي تمّي—ما عم فيّي إتنفّس—ماما بتشدّْ—حاسّة حالي حَموت—الزّلمة المسلّح بِفلّ: وباخد نفس.

I inhale the pool of blood seeping beyond the counter. I inhale my salty tears and the screaming and the crying. But I never breathe again.

بِتنشّق الدّم اللّي عم يِكرُج عالأرض. بتنشّق دموعي المالحة والصّريخ والبكي. بس ما بْعود بتنفّس.

Until I meet her.

لحدّ ما إلتقي فيها.

MONA enters.

Mona.

منى.

YARA's song ("Ahwak") plays gently in the background.

That night, Mama gives me this song.

هَيْديك اللّيلة، ماما قدّمتلي هالغنيّة.

YARA *begins to dance with herself.* MONA *shadows the movements.*

The music swells into the sounds of the nightclub.

RAMI *and* ZIDAN *enter, another glass of vodka in hand.*

2018 blending with 1978.

ZIDAN: *(speaking loudly over the music)* THAT OVER THERE IS THE OWNER. WE CALL HIM BABA IMAD.

RAMI: COOL!

ZIDAN: WELCOME TO THE VIP LIFE, BABY.

RAMI: *I NEVER THOUGHT IT WOULD BE SO GAY IN THE MIDDLE EAST!*

ZIDAN: *IT'S BECAUSE YOU'RE A FOREIGNER!*

They laugh.

LET'S DANCE!!

They dance. It is a movement that choreographs partying, drinking, crowds, sex, and lust. The music increases in volume as the performers move through the space.

MONA *and* YARA *are beyond space and time. Their movements are ghostlike, light and indirect, antiparallel to* ZIDAN *and* RAMI.

The actors move between one another, and they see each other for a brief moment.

The music dims. YARA *and* MONA *are on campus.*

YARA: I have something for you!

إلك شي معي.

YARA fishes out a cassette from her backpack. She hands it to MONA.

MONA: What is this?

شو؟

ZIDAN: Let's get out of here!

RAMI: Where are we gonna go?

YARA: We don't have gold in our family, but my mother used to play me this song whenever I was afraid.

نحنا ما عنا دهب بالعيْلة. بس ماما كانت تْسمِّعني هالغنيّة لما كنت خاف.

MONA: Yara . . .

يارا . . .

YARA: When you're moving from home to home, you don't take much with you. But a song, she said, you can find it anywhere. You can even sing it.

بس تِنقْلي بيوت كتير ما بتاخدي كتير إشيا معك. بس غنيّة، عَقَوْلِتْها، بتلاقيها وين ما كان. وفيكي حتى تغنّيها.

MONA: Wow . . . Thank you.

أوف . . . مرسي.

ZIDAN: You wanna grab a bite?

RAMI: Sure!

ZIDAN: I know an amazing sandwich shop near the beach.

RAMI: Sounds great—my treat!

ZIDAN: Wow, cute Canadian foreigner *and* a gentleman!

YARA: Mona . . . I've never had a friend like you.

منى . . . ولا مرّة كان عندي رفيقة متلك.

MONA takes the cassette.

MONA: I love this. Thank you.

كتير حلوة. مرسي.

MONA and YARA exit.

SCENE SEVEN
FOREIGN WHIMSY

RAMI and ZIDAN are outside the club. Cars are passing by and crowds of people are walking from club to club; the two are in public.

RAMI: Can I ask you a question?

ZIDAN: Sure.

RAMI: Why a phoenix?

ZIDAN: Good question. I'm not sure anymore.

RAMI: It's a good look.

ZIDAN: Thanks. I do *love* a red gown.

RAMI: It looks like it loves you too.

Beat.

ZIDAN: Once upon a time, I used to believe that a phoenix was a promise of eternity.

RAMI: That's beautiful.

ZIDAN: Mmm—it's bullshit. Maybe I believed in that when I first started all this. But bartending night after night, getting stoned in the day, and the most exciting part of my week is taking shots with my friends before a set—it all becomes a little disillusioning.

RAMI: Why don't you do something else?

ZIDAN: Foreigner, you're adorable. You got that lucky passport that gets you into any country you dream of.

RAMI: You want to leave?

ZIDAN: I think about it like everyone else. But no, I don't think I do. I love this country, but I'm just disappointed. I'm disappointed in the traffic jams, and the politicians, and the garbage, and even the tourism—

RAMI: —am I part of this tourism?

ZIDAN: I'm figuring that out. Most days it's better to just count what little wins you win and get on with it.

RAMI: I think we were meant to meet Fifi.

ZIDAN: I love that journey for you. Are you gonna tell me that the salt in your skin is made from the Mediterranean Sea, too?

RAMI: You're funny.

ZIDAN: And you're . . .

> *ZIDAN scrutinizes RAMI, selecting the next word with precision and profound clarity:*

Cute.

RAMI: Hah—thanks.

> *ZIDAN turns to the street.*

ZIDAN: Taxi!

They exit.

The sounds of an emergency siren blare.

Sounds of war, clashes, and gunfire fill the space.

SCENE EIGHT
SHELTER

1978.

*The sounds become subdued into a silence. The radio is playing a
news report in Arabic.*

MONA: One night, Christian and Muslim forces hold the university in
a lockdown with their clashes, forcing the campus to become our own
self-made prison. We're in the basement shelters; water is distributed
and candles are our only source of light.

وهونيك نهار بْيِشْتِبْكوا قوّات مسلّحة مسلمة ومسيحيّة عبواب الجامعة وبِطَوقوها وبْيِحِجْزونا جوّا
متل المساجين. قاعدين بالملجأ عضوّ الشموع وعم بِتْوَزَّع علينا مي.

YARA: There was an uneven air in the building. At first, a lot of fear, but
as the hours passed, pockets of quiet conversations and laughter emerged.

كان الجوّ مْكَرْكَبْ بالمبنى. بالأوّل كان في كتير خوف، بعدين شوي شوي بلّش يطلع صوت أحاديث
عالواطي ومن الأحاديث يطلع ضحك كل ما قطع الوقت.

The ambient sounds of people living closely together is heard.

It's late into the lockdown and YARA *and* MONA *are off to the side
with candles, in their own private space. They're smoking.*

MONA: I haven't had a chance to call Naseeb. He's gotta be worried sick.

ما صَحَّلي دِقْ لنسيب. بِكون انشغل باله.

YARA: He probably heard about it on the radio.

بِكون عرف من الراديو.

MONA: If I could just call the house—

—لو فيّي بس دِقْ عالبيت

YARA: We'll be able to leave in the morning.

بكرا مُنطلع.

MONA: I hope he's at home.

انشالله يكون بالبيت.

YARA: He'll be all right, quiet down.

ما حَيصير عليه شي. روقي شوي.

MONA: How are you so sure?!

كيف فيكي تعرفي؟

YARA: I've been in worse. Please sit, Mona!

قاطعة بأضرب من هيك. بليز اقعدي منى!

MONA sighs.

Sit . . .

اقعدي . . .

A beat as MONA *sits beside* YARA. *They smoke.*

MONA: You know if anything happens to me, I don't know what he'll do.

بْتعرفي إذا بصرلي شي، ما بعرف شُو بْيعمل.

YARA: I know.

بعرف.

Beat.

MONA: I'm sorry, you're probably just as worried—

سوري، عالأرجح إنتي قلقانة كمان. ما بدّي قَلقِك زيادة.

YARA: Mona, it's okay.

منى، طَوْلي بالك.

MONA: Have you spoken to Karam or your mother?

حكيتي مع كرم أو أمك؟

YARA: I haven't. But I promise you, there's nothing we can do other than wait this out. The men out there will either kill each other or get bored enough and go home.

لأ. بس بأكِّدْلك ما فينا نعمل شي غير إنو نقعد وننطر هون. آخرتها الرّجال اللّي برا يا حَيقتلوا بعض يا حَيِزْهقوا ويفلّوا عبيوتهن.

MONA: I don't understand how you're so brave right now.

ما عم بفهم كيف فيكي تكوني هلقد شجاعة هلق.

YARA: I'm not brave. I'm just tired.

ماني شجاعة. تعبانة.

> MONA *takes a beat, still anxious.*

You make this face when you're anxious—I notice it every time.

بتعملي هيك بوجهك بس تِتْوتّري—بلآحظه كل مرة.

MONA: What face?

شو بعمل؟

YARA: *(points at MONA)* That face.

هيك.

MONA: I'm not doing anything—

ما عم بعمل شي—

YARA: It's endearing.

مهضوم.

MONA: Whatever—

أوكي—

YARA: Like this:

هيك:

YARA *mimics* MONA's *face.*

MONA *laughs.*

MONA: You look stupid.

شكلك بِضحِّك.

YARA: Case in point.

بالظبط.

MONA: You said I look cute—

قلتي إنو حلو—

YARA: I said endearing!

قلت مهضوم!

They laugh.

Beat. They continue smoking.

MONA: Yara, what do you think of Naseeb moving us to the mountains?

يارا، شو رأيك بإنو نسيب بدو يانا نطلع عالجبل؟

Beat.

YARA: I think it's a good idea.

بعتقد إنو فكرة منيحة.

MONA: Really?

عنجد؟

YARA: Yes, it's very rare to come by.

إيه، حظكن حلو عندكن أرض بالجبل. ما بتصير كتير هي.

MONA: Huh . . . I thought you would want me to stay.

مم . . . فكرت حتقوليلي بدك ياني ضل.

YARA: I do want you to stay, but it is safer up there.

بدي ياكي تضلي، بس أءمن فوق.

MONA: You know I won't be able to see you.

بتعرفي إنو حيبطل فيّي شوفك.

YARA: I know—

بعرف—

MONA: —you won't be able to see me.

—وحتبطلي تشوفيني.

YARA: Mona—

منى—

MONA: You're okay with that?

ما عندك مشكلة؟

YARA: It's better up there. Karam and I can even help the two of you move.

فوق أحسن. أنا وكرم فينا نساعدكن بالنقلة إذا بدكن.

Beat.

MONA: Karam.

كرم.

YARA: Yes. What's gotten into you?

إيه. شو صارلك؟

MONA: How can you send me off so easily?

كيف فيكي تقليلي فلّي هيك بهالسهولة؟

YARA: In the interest of your safety—

لأنو بدي سلامتك—

MONA: I want to finish this degree . . .

بدي خلّص هالشهادة . . .

Beat.

With you.

معك.

You want me to go into the mountains, then what?

بدّك ياني أطلع عالجبل وبعدين شو؟

YARA: Then you live.

بعدين بتعيشي.

MONA: What life? You all sound the exact same. Naseeb—he's out half these nights with Tarik. He comes home drunk out of his mind and that man fills his head with these stupid ideas. He doesn't want to move to the mountain. I know he doesn't. But whatever Tarik says, he thinks it's the word of God.

أيّ عيشة؟ كلكن بتقولوا ذات الشي. نسيب—مقضّيلي ياها بآخر هالليّالي مع طارق. بْيِرجع عالبيت سكران وما باقي براسه عقل وهالزلمة ما في غير بِعَبّيلو براسه أفكار بلا طعمة. هو ما بدو يطلع عالجبل أنا بعرفه، ما بدو. بس شو ما يقلّو طارق كأنو مُنْزَل.

Look, I'm gonna stay here and I'm gonna finish this degree and it's gonna take a fucking earthquake to unroot me.

ليكي أنا باقية هون وحخلّص شهادتي. ولو هزّت فيّي الأرض ماني متزحزحة.

YARA: Mona . . .

منى . . .

MONA: What're you so afraid of?

من شو خايفة؟

Beat.

YARA: Don't ask for more than what the world will give you—

—ما تطلبي أكتر من ما الحياة بتعطيكي—

MONA: The world will give me what I plant in it.

الحياة حتعطيني شو أنا بزرع فيها.

YARA: What do you even want to do once you leave?

شو بدك تعملي أصلًا بس تْفلّي؟

MONA: *Then* I can live. On my own terms, Yara. Then I can live however I want, with whoever I want.

ساعتها فيني عيش. عذوقي، يارا. متل ما أنا بدي، مع مين ما بدي.

I can live like the French movies!

فيني عيش متل بالأفلام الفرنسيّة.

YARA: —oh goodness—

—يي عليّي أنا—

MONA: With the large windows and endless hills. You know what I'm talking about? I'd have these lavish curtains—

مع شبابيك كبار وجبال عَمَدُّ عينك والنّظر، بتعرفي عن شو عم بحكي؟ حيكون عندي هول البرادي الشيك—

YARA: —of course you would—

—إيه أكيد إيه—

MONA: —with cerulean blue and royal purple trimming. I dream of a home that sits on the highest mountain and it'll have an incredible golden door to welcome me every day—can you imagine, Yara? Being with your lover, sitting in an armchair that's too small for either of you. Reading and laughing and resting and all the afflictions of this fucking war will become a distant memory.

—مْزَرْكَشين لونهن أزرق سماوي وموف ملوكي. عم بِحلم بِبيت عراس أعلى جبل إلو باب ضخم دَهَبي بْيِفْتَحْلي وبأهّل فيّي كل يوم—عم تِتْخايلي يارا؟ تْكوني مع اللّي بتحبّيه، قاعدين عكنباية صغيرة أَنْجَأ سايْعِتْكن. عم تقروا وتضحكوا وتْرَيْحوا وكل أوجاع هالحرب الخرا بتصير ذكرى بعيدة.

More than anything, when I leave, I want to be with someone who I love very much.

أهم شي إنو بس فلّ من هونْ رح كون مع حدا بحبّو كتير.

YARA: The tall rich man?

الرّجال الطويل الغني؟

MONA: Maybe.

يمكن.

YARA: Mona . . .

منى . . .

MONA: It can all happen.

كلّو بصير.

Beat.

YARA: You really believe anything is possible, don't you?

إنتي عنجد بِتآمني إنو أيّ شي ممكن يصير؟

MONA: Yes.

إيه.

YARA: You're crazy, you know that?

مجنونة إنتي، بتعرفي؟

MONA: Oh yes.

إيه بعرف.

YARA: I like that about you.

بحبّ هالشّي فيكي.

Shift.

The two women fall asleep.

The sound of waves lapping nearby and a sparsely busy street rise.

Shift.

SCENE NINE
WHERE PAST AND PRESENT DEPART

2018.

Outside the sandwich shop, near the sea.

RAMI *and* ZIDAN *enter.*

RAMI *holds up the shawarma sandwiches.*

RAMI: Food's ready.

ZIDAN: Thanks . . .
Have you ever had a shawarma?

RAMI: I live in Canada, not under a rock.

ZIDAN: Well, you haven't had a Beiruti shawarma. It's basically a rite of passage to get one when you're out late in this city.

RAMI: Does this mean I'm no longer a foreigner?

ZIDAN: Not yet, Foreigner. But I think I figured you out.

RAMI: All right.

ZIDAN: You're a spy and you're here to investigate the gay life, aren't you?

RAMI: Wow, what gave it away?!

ZIDAN: How far are you willing to go for this role?

RAMI: All the way.

They kiss, quickly, looking around to make sure no one saw them.

ZIDAN: Do you have to kill me now, Mr. Spy?

RAMI: I just might. You have a wild imagination, don't you—

ZIDAN: I need it to thrive, baby.

Shift.

But for real . . . what's your story?

RAMI: Well I'm not a spy.

ZIDAN: I coulda sworn—

RAMI: And I'm totally out—

ZIDAN: —ahh—

RAMI: And I'm almost an architect.

ZIDAN: Oooh . . . sexy . . . almost an architect.

RAMI: My father always wanted me to be an engineer, but it wasn't for me. If it were up to me, I would have been a painter.

ZIDAN: My father wanted me to be a doctor. I became a queen instead.

RAMI: And you're very good at it.

ZIDAN: Thank you so much, habibi.

They kiss again, their inhibitions dropping. Then they release.

I like you.

RAMI: I like you too.

They kiss again.

You know I once dated a Palestinian guy.

ZIDAN: . . . Is that right?

RAMI: His name was Issa, like—Jesus in Arabic.

ZIDAN: I'm familiar with her work.

RAMI: He's part of the reason why I came out to my family. I mean, I was literally dating Jesus from Palestine—I felt pretty invincible.

ZIDAN: Mhmm—

RAMI: Until he cheated on me. And you'd think it would be my mom, but it was my dad who heard me through all of it. He never had the right words, but I always felt I could come to him. And one day, I'm on this huge rant about Issa, cursing his name through these heavy sobs, and Dad just listens; his eyes are like moons, their gravity holding every part of me.

ZIDAN: Rami, this is an uncomfortable amount of talk about our fathers while we're making out.

RAMI: I'm sorry, it's on my mind tonight.

ZIDAN: Well if that isn't the quickest way to kill a boner.

RAMI: Zidan . . .

ZIDAN: Yes?

RAMI: Can you tell me about the war?

Beat.

ZIDAN: What?

RAMI: The civil war. What do you know about it?

ZIDAN: It ended. The end. What more do you want to know?

RAMI: Would you take me to the Green Line?

Beat. ZIDAN *is uncomfortable.*

ZIDAN: What is this about?

RAMI: I need to go the Green Line.

ZIDAN: Don't ask these sorts of questions—

RAMI: Zidan.

ZIDAN: You're being a real *foreigner* right now.

RAMI: I'm sorry—I just—

ZIDAN: —you know what. This was a bad idea.

ZIDAN *begins to exit.*

RAMI: Zidan!

ZIDAN: I'm gonna go home.

RAMI: Waitwaitwait—

ZIDAN: WhatsApp me sometime!

RAMI: —please just WAIT!

ZIDAN: What is going on with you?!

RAMI: I buried my father today!

ZIDAN: *(small)* . . . what?

RAMI: His funeral was today . . .

ZIDAN: That's why you're here . . .

RAMI: Yes.

ZIDAN: Oh man . . . I'm so sorry.

RAMI: This is so fucked up. What am I even doing out?

ZIDAN: Why do you want to go to the Green Line?

RAMI: He never so much as spoke of this place. He didn't even teach me Arabic. But then he wants to be buried here.

RAMI *pulls out a necklace and a photograph.*

He left me these.

ZIDAN: Rami—

RAMI: He wrote here: "Return the necklace to the apartment in this photograph. Find it where Independence meets Damascus, over-looking where the Green Line once ran." Then there's something written in Arabic . . . look.

ZIDAN: Naseeb. It says Naseeb, 1978.

RAMI: That's his name. Naseeb.

Shift.

Beyond space and time.

MONA and YARA stir to life.

MONA: After what happened at the university, Naseeb lost his mind.

بعد اللّي صار بالجامعة، جنّ جنونه نسيب.

NASEEB: NO MORE! WE'RE LEAVING, THIS ISN'T A CONVERSATION!—

خلص بقا! فالّين يعني فالّين. ما في نقاش!—

MONA: He yells like a volcano. I can't suppress him; I can't yell as loudly. I need to finish school! I need to leave this place! I need to find a new home! I need to be with her—

بْيولَع متل البركان. ما فيني هدّيه، وما فيني صرِّخ متلو. بدّي خلّص جامعة! بدّي فلّ من هون! بدّي لاقي بيت جديد! بدّي كون معها—

YARA: —we can't let this grow—

—ما فينا نخلّي هالشّي يكبر—

MONA: —I can't be without her—

—ما فيني كون بعيدة عنها—

YARA: —it won't end well—

—ما حَتِخْلَص منيح—

MON: —I can't breathe without her—

—ما فيني إتنفّس بلاها—

YARA: —not well at all—

—ما حَتِخْلَص منيح أبدًا—

Shift.

1978.

At the university.

MONA: He won't pay this term's tuition! I told him he can go without me. I'm not leaving the apartment!

ما حَيِدْفَعْلي القسط! قلتلّو فيك تْفلَّ بلايي، ما رح أترك الشقة!

YARA: No no no, Mona, you'll go with him!

لا لا لا منى رح تروحي معه!

MONA: I can't be without you.

ما فيني أتركك.

YARA: Are you out of your mind?

جَنَّيْتي؟

MONA: Stop it, Yara! Stop it!

خلص يارا! خلص!

YARA: You don't have a choice.

ما عندك خيار.

MONA: —you're acting like—

—عم تِتْصرّفي كأنو—

YARA: Like what?!

كأنو شو؟!

MONA: Like you don't . . . you're acting like we're only friends.

كأنو مانِك . . . كأنّو نحنا بس رفقة.

YARA: You're truly out of your mind.

لا جَنَّيْتي بالمرّة.

MONA: No!

أ!

YARA: I'm getting married next month.

عم بتجوّز شهر الجاية.

MONA: No . . .

لا . . .

YARA: Mona.

منى.

MONA: When you speak to me, you look at me . . . really look at me . . . like you're seeing my fucking heart beating in my eyes. This war doesn't mean anything when you're here. I know you know that—

بس تحكي معي، بس تِطلَّعي فيّي . . . بس عنجد تِطلَّعي فيّي . . . كأنو عم تشوفي قلبي عم بِدِقْ بعيوني. بتعرفي هالحرب ما كأنها حرب بس كون معك. بعرف إنك بتعرفي—

YARA: Stop it—

—خلص

MONA: With everyone else, you're stern. You're unflinching. But with me you share your cigarettes. With me you speak, you tell me your heart.

مع الكلّ إنتي هيك. عالقَدُّ. بس معي، بِتْشاركيني سواجيرك. معي بْتِحْكي، بْتِحْكي من قلبك.

YARA: Enough . . .

خلص . . .

MONA: I don't want to go . . .

ما بدّي روح . . .

MONA *begins to cry.*

I don't want to leave you.

ما بدّي أتركك.

YARA: Mona . . .

منى . . .

YARA holds MONA.

MONA kisses YARA. Then YARA pushes her away.

WHAT THE FUCK ARE YOU DOING?!?

شو مْفكرة حالك عم تعملي؟!؟

MONA: Yara . . .

يارا . . .

YARA: You're insane!

مجنونة!

YARA begins to exit.

MONA: Yara, wait—please!

يارا انطري—بليز!

YARA: Don't ever speak to me again! You're sick!

ما بَقا بحياتك تحكي معي! مريضة!

You sick woman!

وحدة مريضة!

YARA exits.

Beyond space and time.

ZIDAN sees MONA.

MONA exits.

ZIDAN exits.

SCENE TEN
WEDDING

Beyond space and time.

NASEEB enters.

NASEEB: After what happened at the university, we had to leave. It was too dangerous. She was being careless. And I was a little boy, afraid in those days, but she was intoxicated with her studies. I was the one walking through the veins of our city. I was the one asked to take a gun and stand at the edge of the trenches.

بعد اللّي صار بالجامعة، كان صار لازم نفلّ. كان الوضع كتير خطر وهيّي عم تصير متهورة. وأنا كنت صغير، خايف بهيديك الإيّام، بس هيّي كانت مُشَرْدَقَة بالجامعة وبِعِلْمَها. أنا اللّي كنت عم ببرم بشوارع المدينة، أنا اللّي انْطلب منّي إحمل سلاح وأوقف عبواب الخنادق.

One day, we hear of a potential attack from a group in the Achrafieh. They would come with their crosses swung around their necks—they wanted to kill Anwar—a personal assault. Ammo Tarik asked me to stand guard at the far edge the city—I'd never even shot a gun. I stand, pressed against the sandbags like they are the gloved hands of the earth holding onto my body. After five hours in the sun, I hear movement coming from the line.

هونيك نهار منسمع إنّو في احتمال يصير هجوم بالأشرفية. إنو في مجموعة مسيحيّة بدهن يقتلوا أنور—إعتداء مستهدف يعني. عمّو طارق طلب مني أحرس طرف بعيد من المدينة—وأنا ما بحياتي حامل سلاح. وقفت، لاقي حالي عكياس الرّمل كأنهن راحات الأرض اللّي مهديّة جسمي. بعد شي ٥ ساعات بالشّمس، بسمع حركة جاية من صوب الخط.

My trembling hands take aim. I don't know this weapon. My breathing is sharp—my mind is contorting into unfamiliar shapes—my vision blurs—I can only hear my heart beat—I can only feel the red flush of my heavy lungs—

إيديّي عم يرجفوا، بِصَوْبوا عالصّوت، مش فهمانُه هالسّلاح. نَفَسي قاسي—راسي عم بِروح محلات ما فهمانها—غباش بعيوني—وعم بسمع صوت دقّات قلبي—حاسِس بروايايي عم يغسّلهن دم حامي متل الجمر.

Then: a group of teenagers emerge from the foliage. One screams, "Please—please—please, sir—please, sir, we were just playing—please."

بيطلعوا كم ولد من ورا الشّجر. واحد عم بصرّخ. «دخيلك دخيلك أستاذ كنا بس عم نلعب. الله يخليك. الله يوفقك.».

Beat.

"Get the fuck out of here." And they run away from me.

«فلّوا من هون.» وبيركضوا بعيد.

The attack from the Achrafieh never even comes.

وهجوم الأشرفيّة ما بصير.

Beat.

NASEEB *exits.*

Shift.

1978.

YARA *enters alone.*

Karam and YARA's *wedding. The illustrious wedding spans the entire Green Line, the entire stage, the entire theatre, and the entire world.* YARA's *song is playing and the sounds of wedding cheers, bells, and celebrations are heard. Dancing, feasting, friends, and family, mostly Karam's.*

The music crescendos into a piercing and vibrating hum. The wedding warps and twists, and YARA *is alone, empty.*

Silence. Only a high, dim ringing sound is left in the air.

She exits.

SCENE ELEVEN
BROKEN BREAD

1978.

MONA enters. She is at the apartment. Music plays softly on the radio.

She sweeps, cleans the space, arranges food on the table.

NASEEB enters. He's carrying a bag of bread, a rare commodity in this time of war.

He notices the spread of food.

NASEEB: What's the occasion?

شو المناسبة؟

MONA: Can't I make you dinner anymore?

لازم يكون في مناسبة لحضّرلك أكل؟

NASEEB: You haven't all month.

ما حضّرتي شي إلك شهر.

MONA: Forgive me—

ما تواخذني.

Please. Sit. Let's eat, I'm starving.

بليز اقْعد. خلّينا ناكل مِتّ من الجوع.

NASEEB joins MONA at the table.

He places the bag of bread on the table.

MONA: Oh my God—Naseeb, where did you get this?

نسيب. من وين جبتهن؟

NASEEB: It's yours.

جبتهن إلك.

They eat. Silence.

There are rumours of an Israeli invasion coming from the south.

عم بِقولوا في اجتياح إسرائيلي جاية من الجنوب.

MONA: There are always rumours of an Israeli invasion.

دايمًا في إشاعات عن اجتياح إسرائيلي.

NASEEB: This is serious. Some are saying it might come up to Beirut.

هالمرّة عنجد. عم بِقولوا يِمكن يوصل لبيروت.

MONA: They're just rumours, Naseeb. Don't believe everything
you hear—

إشاعات نسيب. ما تصدّق كل شي بْتسمعه.

NASEEB: I've given it a lot of thought. I know you want to stay, but our
life in the apartment is gonna become impossible. And I'm sorry to
stop paying this semester's tuition. I really am. But we are moving to
the mountain. I saw the plot of land today.

فكّرت كتير. بعرف إنك حابّة تبقي هون بس حياتنا بالشّقة حتصير مستحيلة. سوري إنو ما دفعتلِّك القسط. عنجد بعتذر. بس قرّرت إنو حَننقل عالجبل. شفت شقفة الأرض اليوم.

MONA: That's where you got the bread?

جبت الخبز من هونيك؟

NASEEB: Yes. I understand this isn't what you hoped—

فهمان مش هيدا اللّي كان بدّك ياه.

MONA: Naseeb, I don't think you do understand.

لا نسيب ما بظنّ إنك فهمان.

NASEEB: Then explain it to me.

فسريلي لكان.

MONA: You see that chair over there. Do you remember how Baba used to read to us? Mama would always tell him, "Khalas, they have to go to sleep," and he'd say, "One more page" then read us ten more pages. Do you remember that?

شايف هَيْ الكرسي هونيك؟ بْتتذكّر كيف كان بابا يقعد عليها ويقرالنا قصص؟ ماما تقلّو «خلص صار لازم يفوتوا يناموا» وهو يقلْها «صفحة بعد» ويقوم يقرا عشرة. بتتذكّر؟

NASEEB: I do.

بتذكّر.

MONA: And your favourite book—what was it?

أكتر كتاب بتحبّو—شو كان إسمو؟

NASEEB: *As-Sindubad Al-Bahriya.*

السّندباد البحريّ.

MONA: *As-Sindubad Al-Bahriya,* exactly. You wanted, more than anything, to be Sindubad because he would hook onto the largest bird in existence and fly to Mount Qaf—

إيه، السّندباد البحريّ. كان بدك تكون سندباد من أنت وصغير لأنو كان يتعلّق بأكبر طير ويطير عجبل قاف—

NASEEB: The highest place on earth.

أعلى مطرح عالأرض.

MONA: That's right. And now you want to go to the Chouf because you think it's the highest place on earth. But it's not—

بالظّبط. وهلّق بدّك تروح عالشّوف لأنّك مفكرُه أعلى مطرح عالأرض. بس مانو—

NASEEB: You're being reckless, Mona—

عم تتهوّري منى—

MONA: Say the invasion happens in the south. Say they come in through the farms and fields and work their way up the coast and into Beirut. Say they get into Beirut. Is that where it stops?

فرضنا غزوا الجنوب. فرضنا فاتوا من المزارع وطلعوا عالسّاحل لحدّ بيروت. فرضنا وصلوا عبيروت. حيوقفوا هونيك؟

NASEEB: It's safer up—

—أءمن فوق

MONA: —let me finish. You're worried about Israel? What about what's already happening all around us? Every militia group splinters into smaller factions, each unit becomes ten new ones, brothers eating their brothers' throats. The Chouf is safe right now. But what happens if it isn't tomorrow?

—خلّيني خلّص. خايف من إسرائيل؟ طيّب واللّي عم بصير حوالينا؟ كلّ مليشيا بْتنقسم فصايل، وكلّ فصيلة بتعمل عشرة، أخوة عم بقتلوا بعض. الشّوف آمن هلق. بس شو بصير لمّا بكرا يبطّل آمن؟

NASEEB: We can figure it out then—

—ساعتها الله بْيِفْرِجْها

MONA: No. No, ya albi, you've got it wrong. I have an opportunity here. I am so close to finishing my degree. Then I can build many homes. Naseeb, I imagine we can go much higher than the Chouf; I'll build castles in the clouds. Just let me finish my degree.

لا. لا يا قلبي. مانّك حاسبها صح. أنا هون عندي فرصة. قرّبت كتير خلّص وإتخرّج. وبعدين فيني عمّر بيوت. نسيب، فينا نطلع كتير أعلى من الشّوف؛ رح عمّر قْصور بالغيوم. بس خلّيني إتخرّج.

NASEEB: And what if you get killed on campus?

وإذا انْقَتَلْتي بالجامعة؟

MONA: I haven't so far—

—بعدني عايشة لهلّق

NASEEB: Mona.

منى.

MONA: Then I die.

ساعتها بموت.

NASEEB: I can't let them hurt you . . .

ما فيني خلّيهن يأذوكي . . .

MONA: Who?

مين؟

Beat. Silence.

NASEEB: It's good in the mountains. It's so beautiful and there are many good men you can marry.

الوضع منيح بالجبل. المنطقة حلوة وفي كتير رجال أوادم بتلاقي حدا وبتتجوّزيه.

Beat.

MONA: I'm not going.

ماني رايحة.

NASEEB: Yes, you are.

مبلا، رايحة.

MONA: I've spoken to Mr. Said. He said I can take the job at the store.

حكيت معلّم سعيد. وقالي إنو فيّي آخد الشّغل عندو بالمحل.

NASEEB: You spoke to Mr. Said again?

رجعتي حكيتي مع معلّم سعيد.

MONA: I'll work in the evenings—

حإشتغل المسا—

NASEEB: What has gotten into you?

شو صايرلِك؟

MONA: I'll be able to attend classes in the—

وبحضر صفوفي بال—

NASEEB: You want to work in the evenings like some fucking slut?

بدّك تشتغلي المسا متل وحدة فلتانة؟

MONA: Naseeb!

نسيب!

NASEEB: Absolutely not. Don't ever go behind my back again—can you imagine what people are gonna say?!

أكيد لأ. وما بَقا بحياتك تحكي حدا من ورا ضهري—عم تتخايلي العالم شو بدها تقول!

MONA: I don't give a fuck what people will say.

آخر همّي العالم شو بِتقول.

NASEEB: Maybe you should!

يمكن لازم يهمّك!

    MONA stands.

MONA: I'm taking the job. I wasn't asking. I was informing you. You can go to the mountains; you can stay there and worry about the rumours and the invasions all you like. I'll be here.

رح آخد الشّغل. ما كنت عم بسألك. كنت عم خبرك. فيك تطلع عالجبل تقعد هونيك تعتل همّ الإشاعات والإجتياحات قد ما بدّك. أنا حكون هون.

NASEEB: No you won't.

لا ما حتكوني هون.

I found a buyer for the apartment.

دبّرت بَيْعِة الشقة.

Silence.

MONA *exits.*

The sounds of a city in the night and the lapping of waves from the nearby sea.

SCENE TWELVE
SHIFTING

2018.

Overlooking the sea, near the sandwich shop.

ZIDAN enters.

ZIDAN: Mama is Muslim and Baba is Christian . . . the Green Line took a lot of our family. I don't know that war, Rami.

RAMI: I'm sorry—

ZIDAN: So please excuse me if I don't want to talk about it.

RAMI: I leave in a week.

ZIDAN: So you have a week to fulfill his wishes.

RAMI: I don't know how to do this, Zidan.

ZIDAN: I'm sorry about this. But don't ask me to help you—the Green Line dissolved into the sea, the buildings were torn down, rebuilt, everything was uprooted. The apartment is probably not even standing anymore.

RAMI: A point in the right direction would help.

ZIDAN: Are you even listening to me?

RAMI: Zidan—

ZIDAN: No! You're pushing your luck, Foreigner. Put this to rest for tonight.

RAMI: I'm trying.

ZIDAN: Why tonight?

RAMI: Because I don't want to deal with this! I don't want to do this, Zidan! I don't want any of his past. It's *HIS* past. I don't even want to be here. This isn't my place; this isn't my home; this is not my war. He told us to never return, to never ask about it, and to never even *THINK* of this place. And then he wants to be buried here?! What the actual fuck?! And this necklace—and this photograph. Why? Why is he doing this? Why now?

ZIDAN: So you went to a gay club instead?

RAMI: Yes! Because it's the only place I could think right.

ZIDAN: Rami, we've had a lot to drink right now—this isn't a good time to deal with this—

RAMI: No, this is the best time, frankly.

ZIDAN: Where are you going?

RAMI: To the fucking Green Line.

RAMI begins to exit.

ZIDAN: Rami!

RAMI exits.

Fuck!

Shift.

SCENE THIRTEEN
FOR THE BRIEFEST MOMENT

1978.

Phone ringing.

MONA is in her apartment, phone in hand.

YARA enters her own apartment and answers the phone.

YARA: Hello—

ألو—

MONA: Yara . . .

يارا . . .

Beat.

Please wait.

بليز انطري.

YARA: Why are you calling—

ليه عم تْدِقِّي—

MONA: Wait, don't hang up the phone!

لحظة، ما تْسكري!

YARA: Forget this number, Mona.

انسي هالرّقم منى.

MONA: Congratulations.

مبروك.

YARA: . . .

MONA: Are you still there?

بعدك هون؟

YARA: Yes.

إيه.

MONA: I just wanted to say congratulations . . . on your marriage.

بس كان بدّي قلّك مبروك . . . عالعرس.

YARA: Is that it?

خلّصتي؟

MONA: I know it was this weekend.

بعرف إنو كان هالويكأند.

YARA: Yes.

إيه.

MONA: I mean it, Yara . . . I wish you so many blessings.

بِعنيها يارا . . . بتمنّالِك كل شي منيح.

YARA: Thank you.

مرسي.

MONA: You're welcome.

يا هلا.

They breathe together in silence.

Are you still there?

بعدك هون؟

YARA: Yes.

إيه.

MONA: Okay.

أوكي.

YARA: Okay.

أوكي.

Beat.

MONA: How was it?

كيف كان؟

YARA: Mona—

—منى

MONA: How was the day?

النهار. كيف كان النهار؟

YARA: Karam will be home soon. I have to go—

—كرم حيوصل بأي لحظة. لازم فلّ

MONA: Yara, I'm so sorry—

—يارا بعتذر

YARA: —don't . . .

. . . خلص—

MONA: Please . . . listen to me . . . what happened—what I did—

—بليز . . . اسمعيني . . . اللّي صار—اللّي عملتو

YARA: Forget about it—

—إنسي الموضوع

MONA: I can't!

!ما فيني

YARA: Forget about us—

انسينا—

MONA: You don't mean that.

ما بتعنيها.

YARA: I have to go.

لازم روح.

MONA: I have a bird hanging from my neck—

عندي عصفور معلّق عرقبتي—

YARA: What?

شو؟

MONA: My mother gave me this necklace because it isn't God or Allah or Jesus or anyone who will save me. She gave me this necklace so that I could die a hundred thousand deaths and still come back to life each time.

ماما عطتني هالعقد لأنو لا الله ولا يسوع ولا حدا حيخلّصني. عطتني هالعقد لحتى إذا متت مية موتة إرجع عالحياة كل مرة.

YARA: What are you talking about?

عن شو عم تحكي؟

MONA: She told me to get an education, learn, then leave. And she gave me the wings to leave on.

قالتلي إتعلّم، خلّص علمي، وفلّ. وعطتني جوانح تا طير.

YARA: You are so naive.

ساذجة أنت.

MONA: I never wanted the affections of men . . .

ولا مرة كان بدّي عاطفة الرجال . . .

YARA: With your delusional fables—

بقصصك الخرافيّة—

MONA: I'm not sick.

ماني مريضة.

YARA: You're insane—

مجنونة—

MONA: I've never met a person less afraid of a bullet than her own dreams. You're brave, Yara. Be brave!

ما بحياتي التقيت بحدا بِخاف من أحلامه أكتر من رصاصة. إنتي شجاعة يارا، كوني شجاعة!

YARA: You don't know what's out there—

ما بتعرفي شو في برا—

MONA: Of course I do!

مبلا بعرف!

YARA: No, you really don't!

لا ما بتعرفي!

You don't know what it's like to have Mama wake you in the middle of the night and force you back to a hellhole refugee camp to find Baba's dead body. That's not a story, that's not a fantasy—that's what's real, Mona!

ما بتعرفي شو يعني أمّك تْفَيْقِك بنصّ اللّيل وتردُّك بالقوة عالمخيّم، عجهنّم الحمرا لتلاقي بيّك مقتول. هي مش قصة. مش خرافة—هي الحقيقة منى!

MONA: I know—

بعرف—

YARA: You don't know what it's like to watch the Tigers with their crosses spray bullets into Baba. Into the hearts of all the men in our camp. They said if we so much as cried, we would be next. You don't understand that kind of terror. Or the kind of terror when Mama returns to the mass grave and tills the earth with her bare claws until she finds his body.

ما بتعرفي شو يعني تشوفي النُّمور الأحرار لابسين هالصّلبان وعم بِرشّوا بابا رصاص. عم بِرشّوا كلّ رجال المخيّم. وقال إذا بْكينا بِرشّونا وراهن. ما بتعرفي هالرّعب. أو رعب ماما هي وعم تنبُش قبور بِضَفيرها لتلاقي جثّته.

You don't know what it feels like to sit with the corpse of your father in a rundown truck barrelling through the back roads of this city. She crossed the Green Line like it was a pedestrian crossing—all so she could give him a proper burial. That's all she wanted. That's all she needed. To bury him in a proper grave.

ما بتعرفي شو يعني تقعدي حدّ جثة بيّك بِبيك-أب مهرهرة عم تْخَضْخِض عطرقات المدينة الفرعيّة. قطعِت خطّ التّماس كأنو جسر مشاة ليه؟ لَتِقْدَر تدفنه متل العالم والنّاس. هيدا كلّ اللّي كان بدها ياه. كل شي كان بدها ياه. تْكَرْمُه وتدفنه متل الخلق.

>	*Beat.*

So yes, I marry a living man, although my body aches at the thought, because I am not the only one making this choice.

فإيه بتجوّز رجّال عايش، معإنّو جسمي بيوجعني كل ما فكّر فيها، لأنو ما عم باخد هالقرار وحدي.

MONA: I've buried my own share of death—or did you forget?

أنا كمان اختبرت الموت—ولّا نسيتي؟

YARA: Did *you*?

إنتي نسيتي؟

MONA: No. I just started to believe there might be some life again when I met you.

لا. بس رجعت آمن إنو بَرْكي في حياة بعد ما التقيت فيكي.

>	*Beat.*

The apartment's been sold and we're moving to the mountains. I'm sure they'll marry me to someone soon.

الشّقة انْباعت ورح نِطلع عالجبل. وأكيد حَيْجَوْزوني لحدا كمان عن قريب.

YARA: Oh no . . .

يي لا . . .

>	*Beat.*

MONA: For a single moment, I truly believed a different future was imaginable. With you, I thought we could go somewhere far away and start over. We would make it our way—we are the builders of homes. Isn't that right? Am I crazy? Am I?

بتعرفي للحظة قدرت إتخايل مستقبل تاني كان ممكن يصير. معك، فكّرت إنو فينا نروح شي محلّ بعيد ونبلّش عن جديد. ونعمل كلّ شي عذوقنا. نحنا منعمّر بيوت. ماهيك؟ عم هلوس؟ أنا؟ عم هلوس؟

I don't think I am.

ما بظنّ.

But it was as if you were a bubble, Yara . . . and all of it has vanished into the air.

بس كأنّو كنتي وهم يارا . . . فُقاعة . . . وفقعت بالهوا.

> MONA *hangs up.*

> MONA *curls to sleep by the phone.*

> YARA *lingers . . . then hangs up.*

> YARA *exits.*

SCENE FOURTEEN
A GROWING GREEN LINE

Beyond space and time.

NASEEB enters.

He watches his sister from afar. She is curled around the phone.

Suddenly, a piercing gunshot reverberates through the air.

Shift.

1978.

NASEEB is shot in the shoulder—he screams in pain. As his voice fades, YARA's song slowly rises into the space.

MONA stirs to life where she had been asleep.

Time passes. NASEEB places his arm in a shoulder sling.

He enters the apartment. The song plays softly on the radio.

Shift.

MONA: Bismillah al Rahman al Raheem! *[Oh my God!]* Naseeb, what happened?

باسم الله الرّحمن الرّحيم. نسيب شو صار؟

NASEEB: Nothing—

ماشي—

He heads for his room.

MONA: What's wrong with your shoulder?

شو بو كتفك؟

NASEEB: Nothing!

ماشي!

MONA: Let me see!

فرجيني!

She stops him.

MONA: Oh my God, you were shot?

يا دلِّي! اتْقوّصت؟

NASEEB: It's nothing.

ما بِني شي.

MONA: Who did this? Where have you been? I told you to stay put!

مين عمل فيك هيك؟ وين كنت؟ قلتلّك تبقى هون!

NASEEB: Why haven't you been packing?

ليه مش ضابّة؟

MONA: What did you do?

شو عملت؟

NASEEB: Nothing!
I did nothing.
I was with Ammo Tarik and we walked into the wrong place.
And we're lucky that we only got out with this.
Do you want a bullet in my head before you come with me?

ماشي!
ما عملت شي.
كنت مع عمّو طارق ومشينا بالمحلّ الغلط.
نشكر الله ما صار أكتر من هيك. بدّك إنصاب براسي قبل ما تجي معي؟

MONA: No . . .

لا . . .

NASEEB: We're leaving at the end of this week.

حنفلّ بآخر الأسبوع.

Beat.

MONA: Okay.

أوكي.

NASEEB: If you had listened to me from the beginning, we would have already been in the mountains—but instead you've been sitting around, reading your fucking books! Turn the music off!

لو سمعتي منّي من الأوّل كنّا هلّق صرنا بالجبل—بس قاعدة عم تقري بالكتب! طفّيلي هالموسيقى!

He heads for the radio.

MONA: No, Naseeb—

—لا نسيب

NASEEB: We are *IN A FUCKING WAR.*

نحنا بحرب شرموطة.

MONA: *NASEEB, WAIT!*

نسيب لحظة!

NASEEB: You don't play music, you don't read, you don't study!!!

ما بتسمعي موسيقى، ما بتقري، ما بتدرسي!!!

In a rage, he tears into the radio, into the cassette—

MONA: *WAIT, PLEASE WAIT!*

لحظة بس لحظة!

—and destroys it.

Beat.

Oh my God.

لا يا الله.

NASEEB: *You* did this.

إنتي عملتي هيك.

NASEEB exits.

MONA crumples beside the broken cassette.

Then . . . from a memory . . . ZIDAN enters the space.

ZIDAN approaches MONA and helps her to her feet.

Memories breathe to life. Time and space fractal into infinity.

She smiles at him.

The apartment transforms—MONA dresses ZIDAN in bells, shawls, and a thick, black mascara.

Music plays. They dance. She embraces him.

ZIDAN: I know you . . . this apartment . . . this door. I know this place.

They both exit.

The world returns.

SCENE FIFTEEN
AN ETERNAL KISS

Beyond space and time.

YARA enters.

YARA: We thought we were the engineers, but it turns out they can shape us into whatever they want. He'll marry her off . . . Mona . . . another warrior woman ground down into a mound of sand.

فكّرنا حالنا المهندسين، بس طلع إنّو فيهن يِجِبْلونا عذوقهن. حيجوزوها . . . منى . . . مرا مُناضلة جديدة طحنوها لحتى صارت رمل.

They will cement us into the earth. She always knew that.

حَيْزَفْتونا مع الأرض. كانت بتعرف.

I come home from class and my husband has finished a day at the shop. His hands are blackened with exhaustion.

رْجعت عالبيت من الجامعة وجوزي كان راجَع من المحلّ. إيديه سود من كتر التّعب.

"Yara, my dove, would you please make me some dinner?" "Of course."

«يارا، يا حسونتي بتحضريلنا لقمة طيبة من إيدك؟» «أكيد.»

Mama sits in her room, as always, listening to the radio. Threats of invasions have replaced the melodies of her songs and the names of the martyred and murdered drone into the hallway. She is another mound of sand.

ماما قاعدة بأُوضتها، متل العادة، عم تسمع راديو. تبدّلوا نغمات الأغاني اللّي كانت تسمعهن بتهديدات إجتياح وأسامي الشّهدا والمقتولين وعبّوا الكوريدور. هِيّ كومة رمل جديدة.

I make dinner. I watch television with Karam; he begins to kiss my neck. I retreat to study for the night.

بْحضّر عشا. بِحضَر تلفزيون مع كرم. بِبَلّش يبوس رقبتي. بنسحب لأدرس.

The next day, I come home, I make dinner, the television blowing bombs, the radio droning on. He kisses my neck.

تاني نهار برجع عالبيت، بْحضِّر عشا، قنابل عم تفقع عالتلفزيون، الراديو عم يحكي، بِبوس رقبتي.

The next day, he kisses my neck. The next day, he kisses my arms. The next day, he kisses my chest. He presses himself into my body—he tells me he wants to have a little boy. The next day, the next day, the next day, how many next days before my skin melts into the earth and I harden into its softness?

النهار اللّي بعدو، بِبوس رقبتي. النهار اللّي ورا ببوس إيديّي. واللّي ورا صدري. بِحطّ جسمو عجسمي—بِقلّي يدو نعمل صبي صغير. اليوم اللّي بعدو، واللّي بعدو، واللّي بعدو، كم يوم بعد قبل ما يدوب جسمي بالأرض وإءسى وإجمد بالتراب.

Me? I will become a mound of sand . . .

أنا؟ حَصير كومة رمل . . .

But Mona—she is made of sky.

بس منى—مجبولة من السما.

She's a gift.

هديّة.

1978.

MONA'*s apartment.*

MONA *is packing.*

A knock on the door.

MONA: Coming—

—يلا

She opens the door to find YARA.

Oh my God—

باسم الله—

YARA: Hi, Mona.

هاي منى.

MONA: Yara . . .

يارا . . .

YARA: How are you?

كيفك؟

MONA: What're you doing here?

شو عم تعملي هون؟

YARA: I wanted . . . I needed . . . to see you.

كنت بدّي . . . كنت بحاجة . . . شوفك.

MONA: Are you okay?

بكي شي؟

YARA: Is your brother home?

خيّك بالبيت؟

MONA: He stepped out . . .

ضهر . . .

MONA: Come . . . come in—

فوتي—

YARA: No, thank you . . .

لا مرسي . . .

MONA: Are you okay?

بكي شي؟

YARA: I'm fine.

أنا منيحة.

MONA: How is Karam?

كيفو كرم؟

YARA: He's good.

منيح.

Beat.

MONA: Yara, this is strange . . . to see you.

يارا . . . غريب إنّو . . . شوفك.

YARA: Tell me something . . . do you *want* to go the mountains?

قليلي . . . بدّك تطلعي عالجبل؟

MONA: What?

شو؟

YARA: Tell me. Please. Tell me what your life will look like?

جاوبيني. بليز. قليلي كيف حَيكون شكل حياتك؟

MONA: I don't know . . .

ما بعرف . . .

YARA: The mountains *are* beautiful. It'll give you some quiet, right?

الجبل حلو. رواق، ما هيك؟

MONA: So I keep being told—why does it feel like it'll bring me the opposite?

إيه هيك بِضلّهن يقولوا—ليه حاسّة إنو حَيكون كل شي إلا رواق؟

YARA: Mona . . . I care about you a lot.

منى . . . بْتعنيلي كتير.

Beat.

What you said—on the phone . . .

اللّي قلتيه عالتلفون . . .

MONA: Why are you here?

ليه جيتي؟

YARA: They'll marry you off . . . and you'll live a quiet life.

حَيْجَوْزوكي . . . وتْعيشي حياة رايقة.

MONA: I'm making some peace with it—

عم بِتْقبّل الموضوع—

YARA: I started imagining *you* in a quiet life . . . That's not a life at all. Where would all your wonder fit?

بلّشت إتخايلك بحياة رايقة . . . هَيْ مش حياة. وين بتروحي بدهشتك وأحلامك؟

MONA: Are you here to hurt me?

جاية تأذيني؟

YARA: When I feel the weight of Karam on my body, it's like a rock is pressed against my chest. This gentle man becomes a giant when we share a bed.

بس حسّ بِتِقِل كرم عجسمي، كأنو في بْلاطة قاعدة عصدري. هالرجّال الرقيق بْيِتْحَوّل لَشي ضخم وتْقيل بس نِتشارك تخت.

MONA: Yara.

يارا.

YARA: I wish I never met you.

ياريت ما التقيت فيكي.

MONA: What are you doing?

شو عم تعملي؟

YARA: I wish I never met you because I don't know how I'll ever go back to being without you. I can't imagine what is waiting for you—

يا ريت بحياتي ما التقيت فيكي لأنو ما بقا أعرف إرجع للحياة من قبلك. ما قادرة إتخايل شو اللّي ناطرك—

MONA: I'll take care of myself.

ما تعتلي همّ. بْدير بالي عحالي.

YARA: Imagining you in a quiet life—who will they marry you to?

عم بتخايلك بحياة رايقة—مين حَيْجَوْزوكي؟

MONA: —what is wrong with you?—

—شو صايرلك؟—

YARA: Someone terrible.

واحد مش منيح.

MONA: Please leave.

بليز فلِّي.

YARA: I can't leave you. I won't.

ما فيني أتركك. ما رح أتركك.

There is a lot I can stay silent about but the weight of your life in those mountains is more devastating than anything this war can bring.

في كتير إشيا فيني أسكت عنها بس حياتك بالجبل أَتْقَل من أيّ شي عملتُه هالحرب.

I started imagining you and I—together . . .

عم بِتْخايَلنا . . . سوا . . .

MONA: You said I was a sick woman.

قلتي عني مريضة.

YARA: I was wrong.

غْلطت.

MONA: Wha . . .

شو . . .

YARA: This—us—I've never felt more healed with you. You . . . your spirit makes air out of stones . . . and you know the stones I've swallowed in my life.

هيدا الشّي، نحنا، ما في شي بِحسِّسني إني منيحة، إني صحّ متل لمّا كون معك. إنتي، روحك بِتْحَرِّك الحجر . . . وبتعرفي الحجار اللي بَلَّعتني ياهن الحياة.

MONA: What do you want, Yara?

شو بدّك يارا؟

YARA: Let's run away.

خلّينا نهرب.

MONA: What?

شو؟

YARA: Through the Green Line . . . through the mountains. Through the deserts and the seas. We'll say goodbye to everything and everyone we know, and we'll start somewhere else.

من قلب خطّ التّماس. من قلب الجبل. من قلب الصّحرا والبحر. مِنْوَدِّع كل شي وكل حدا مْنعرفه، ومِنبلّش عن جديد بمطرح جديد.

MONA: Are you crazy?

جَنَّيْتي؟

YARA: Yes.

إيه.

MONA: Yara, what're you talking about?

يارا شو عم تحكي؟

YARA: I'll help you move. I'll help you move to the mountain, that's what we'll say. Once we make it to the Chouf and everyone is sleeping, we will leave in the middle of the night.

بْساعدِك تنقلي عالجبل. عم ساعدك بالنّقلة، هيك منقول. وبس نوصل عالشّوف، مِنْفِلّ بْنصّ اللّيل، وقت ما الكلّ يكونوا نايمين.

MONA: To where?

لوين؟

YARA: To Syria, then to Turkey, then to Europe . . . I don't care, you imagine. *You* imagine.

عسوريا، بعدين تركيا، بعدين أوروبا . . . ما بعرف، ما بهمّ. نقّي. إنتي تخايلي ونقّي.

MONA: I have to think about this—

خلّيني فكّر—

YARA: We can start over—

فينا نْبلّش من أوّل وجديد—

MONA: Yara—

—يارا

YARA: I don't want to live without you. I don't want to—the first time I saw you it was as if we looked at each other for a hundred thousand years.

ما بدّي عيش بلاكي. ما بدّي—أول مرّة شفتك، حسّيت كأنو كان إلنا مية ألف سنة عم نتّطلع بعيون بعض.

I love you, Mona. I love you very much and I am so sorry it took me this long to learn it.

بحبّك منى. بحبّك كتير وبعتذر إنّو أخدني هلقد وقت تا أعرف.

YARA kisses MONA.

MONA: We leave at the end of the week.

حنفِلّ بآخر الأسبوع.

NASEEB enters.

NASEEB: Yara.

يارا.

YARA: Hi—   **MONA:** Naseeb!

مرحبا—

نسيب!

NASEEB: I haven't seen you in a while—

زمان ما شفناكي—

YARA: I've been busy.

انْشغلت.

NASEEB: Right—

مم—

MONA: Yara's offered to help us with the move.

يارا عم تعرض تساعدنا بالنقلة.

NASEEB: Thank you.

يسلموا.

YARA: Of course—

وَلَوْ.

NASEEB: How's Karam?

كيفُه كرم؟

YARA: He's good.

منيح.

NASEEB: Good.

منيح.

Beat.

Would you like to come in for dinner?

فوتي تعشّي معنا.

YARA: I've gotta make dinner at home. Thank you.

كلّك ذوق. لازم روح حضّر عشا.

NASEEB: Are you sure—

فوتي.

YARA: Yeah—yeah—I gotta go—I'll see you both later.

لا لا عنجد كلّك ذوق. بشوفكن بعدين.

MONA: Bye. **NASEEB:** Bye.

باي باي. مع السّلامة.

YARA exits.

MONA exits.

SCENE SIXTEEN
BREATHING

ZIDAN rushes in.

ZIDAN: Rami!

RAMI: Zidan?

ZIDAN: *(out of breath)* Hey! Hi! Holy-shit-you-quick-little-minx, you disappeared on me.

RAMI: What are you doing?

ZIDAN: You wanna get to that apartment?

RAMI: What?

ZIDAN pulls out a bottle of beer. He holds it out to RAMI.

I think we've drank enough—

ZIDAN: Please—

RAMI: You're pushy.

ZIDAN: And you're crazy—

RAMI: Wow, thanks.

ZIDAN: Have it. I got one myself.

ZIDAN pulls out another one for himself. He takes a big swig.

I think you're crazy but—

       ZIDAN takes another swig.

But I want to have one more drink with you.

RAMI: No thanks.

ZIDAN: Oh really?—

RAMI: Bye.

       RAMI begins to head off.

ZIDAN: You're going the wrong way, Foreigner.

RAMI: You know what? /

ZIDAN: What?

RAMI: / You're being a condescending asshole, Zidan. You call me a foreigner as if it's cute. You got me all these drinks like you're doing me a favour. /

ZIDAN: Woah, slow down, sweetie— /

RAMI: / You make up all these stories about me, you can't even help me. /

ZIDAN: / —stop stop stop stop stop! Please stop moving your mouth.

RAMI: Wow.

ZIDAN: I'm here to help you—

RAMI: "Please stop moving your mouth." You're an asshole—

ZIDAN: I'm sorry!

RAMI: I had this stupid fucking idea that maybe this was supposed to happen. That we were supposed to meet.

ZIDAN: Rami . . .

RAMI: Over there—across the ocean—I am myself, so singularly myself, I get all the benefits of being by myself. But my parents . . . my father . . . his broken English . . . made me feel like I was a part of something else.

And then he gives me this necklace, and it's a bird, a phoenix. And tonight, I look at you, right after his funeral, and you were dressed like this necklace, and I wanted to believe that maybe all this meant something. That I was in the right place at the right time . . . maybe—maybe I could feel him. That this land keeps him alive somehow, and I don't have to lose him.

ZIDAN: Woah . . .

    Beat.

RAMI: *UGH!*
I am fucking crazy.

    RAMI *picks up the bottle and takes a swig.*

ZIDAN: If you're crazy then so am I.

RAMI: Why?

ZIDAN: I know that apartment.

RAMI: What?

ZIDAN: Can I see the picture again?

RAMI hands ZIDAN the picture.

For sure this is it.

RAMI: You're lying.

ZIDAN: I'm not—

RAMI: . . .

They both take a swig.

ZIDAN: I think you and I were meant to find each other, Rami.

RAMI: Why?

ZIDAN: Because here we are.

RAMI: That doesn't explain anything.

ZIDAN: Maybe it's enough.

RAMI: Maybe we're both drunk.

Shift.

SCENE SEVENTEEN
HOW A SOUL SAYS GOODBYE

Seamless continuity from the previous moment.

1978 blurring with 2018.

MONA enters.

She is on the phone.

The memories come to life, the Green Line alive, breathing, and braiding RAMI, MONA, YARA, and ZIDAN together.

MONA: We're ready to leave.

جاهزين نمْشي.

YARA: Okay.

أوكي.

MONA: You'll help us with the move and Naseeb's agreed to drive you back tomorrow night.

بتساعدينا بالنّقلة ونسيب بِوَصْلِك بكرا باللّيل.

YARA: Okay—

—أوكي

MONA: Tarik will meet us outside the city.

طارق حَيْلاقينا برّات المدينة.

YARA: But when they've fallen asleep, you and I will run—

—وبس يفوتوا يناموا، أنا ويّاكي منهرب

MONA: That's right.

صحّ.

YARA: We'll keep driving?

مِنْكَفِّي سواقة؟

MONA: Yes.

إيه.

More blurring, braiding: beyond space and time, 2018 blurring with 1978.

ZIDAN: Do you trust me?

RAMI: I'm figuring that out.

ZIDAN: That apartment is a safehouse where queer people could gather.

RAMI: What do you mean?

ZIDAN: When my parents found out I was gay, they kicked me out of our home. A good friend told me about this place.

YARA: I'm afraid—

خايفة—

MONA: I'm leaping from the crane—

عم فَلِّت الرّافعة.

YARA: I've only ever known bullets and battered bodies.

ما عرفت غير رصاص وجثث.

MONA: I pray that my wings will hold us both.

وعم بِدعي إنو جناحاتي يحملونا تُنَيْناتنا.

ZIDAN: I stayed there for a year. I couldn't tell from the photo because the door is painted gold now. But I'm sure of it. The way the olive vines wrap along the sides, and those windows.

RAMI: Why is my dad there?

ZIDAN: I'm not sure. But there was a woman who ran the place—

YARA: —how did we get here?—

—كيف وصلنا لهون؟—

MONA: —I've known you for a hundred thousand years—

—عرفتك مية ألف سنة—

YARA: —we said—

—قلنا—

MONA: —we'll run away—

—حنهرب لبعيد—

YARA: —through the Green Line—

—من قلب خطّ التّماس—

MONA: —through the mountains—

—من قلب الجبل—

YARA: —the deserts—

—الصّحرا—

MONA: —and the seas—

—والبحر—

ZIDAN: She took care of all of us. The first place I ever performed in drag was in the living room of that apartment.

RAMI: She knew my dad?

Shift—the Green Line consumes the stage, vines and trees crushing through cement, swelling into a maelstrom of memories.

ZIDAN: She taught me that when a person dies there is always a blackness, a heaviness in the days and weeks that follow as the soul lies in its sleep. When it wakes it does not remember where it is, what it does, and *why* it is. It swims through the channels of the body until it escapes the skin.

YARA: We'll say goodbye to everything and everyone we know—

—حودِّع كلّ شي وكلّ حدا عرفتُه

MONA: —to be with—

—تكون

YARA & MONA: —you—

—معك

MONA: —to feel you—

—تَحسّ فيكي

YARA: —to kiss you—

—تَبوسك

MONA: —to love you—

—تَحبّك

YARA: —I have always loved you—

—حبّيتك من زمان

ZIDAN: The soul floats just above the body, watching and not watching. Dispersed and suspended. Whole and not easily understood. It celebrates and mourns in a celestial dance, swimming in and out of the body. Then . . . it takes its first breath.

Beat.

RAMI: What happens next?

ZIDAN: Some go to another plane immediately; others transmigrate into another body. But some souls wait. They get lodged in the earth, waiting for their freedom. Sometimes, we can see them if we look close enough.

RAMI: Zidan, what is this about?

ZIDAN: Some souls wait, cycling through a lifetime of memories trying to make sense of something.

RAMI: Do you mean he's waiting?

ZIDAN: These souls wait to hear a message or finish an important mission.

RAMI: I could feel him all night.

ZIDAN: I've been so afraid to believe in anything for a long time—and then you show up.

MONA: How long have you been here?

قدّي إلك هون؟

ZIDAN: How long has it been since he left Beirut?

YARA: Forty years.

٤٠ سنة.

RAMI: Forty years.

YARA: I've been here forty years.

إلي ٤٠ سنة هون.

MONA: I remember—

بتذكّر—

YARA: We were running away . . .

كنّا عم نهرب . . .

MONA: I know—

بعرف—

YARA: We were laughing—

كنّا عم نضحك—

MONA: Oh God.

يا الله.

YARA: I remember it all—

بتذكّر كل شي—

MONA: I wish I didn't—

يا ريت ما بتذكّر—

The air is sucked from the space.

Shift: back to that day.

SCENE EIGHTEEN
THE FALL OF NIGHT

Beyond space and time blurring with 1978.

The Green Line contorts, memories becoming hauntings.

MONA: That morning—

صبح هيداك النهار—

YARA: —the air was wet with a heavy fog—

—الجو كان رطب وكان في غْطَيْطة قويّة—

NASEEB: —I was afraid in those days—

—كنت خايف هيديك الأيّام—

MONA: —Yara came to our apartment and helped with the last of the packing—

—إجت يارا لعنّا وقتها وساعدتني ضبّ آخر كم شغلة—

NASEEB: —I was a little boy—

—كنت صغير—

YARA: —and when everything was in the car, I sat in the back seat—

—وبس حطّينا كل شي بالسّيارة، قعدت ورا—

MONA: —it would be the last time I would be with my brother—

—كانت آخر مرّة حَشوف فيها خيّي—

YARA: —and I could see her face in the rear-view mirror—

—وعم شوف وجهها بالمراية—

MONA: —and the last time I would see my childhood home—

—وآخر مرّة بشوف البيت اللّي كبرت وربيت فيه—

NASEEB: —Yara and Mona—

—يارا ومنى—

MONA: —leaving behind memories of Mama and Baba—

—تاركين ذكريات ماما وبابا ورانا—

NASEEB: —I'd heard—

—سمعت—

MONA: —leaving my brother—

—تاركة خيّي—

Shift.

1978.

Outside MONA *and* NASEEB'*s apartment.*

They are preparing to leave in the car.

MONA: Wait wait! Naseeb!—

—لحظة لحظة نسيب!—

NASEEB: What?

شوفي؟

MONA: Stand right there—by the entrance—I want a photo of you.

وُقاف عندك—عالمدخل—بدّي آخدلك صورة.

NASEEB: It's not the time.

مش وقتها هلق.

MONA: Please, we'll do it quickly.

بليز عالسّريع.

NASEEB: Let's go—

—يلا إمشي

MONA: Naseeb, please.

نسيب بليز.

NASEEB: Fine.

طيّب.

NASEEB stands, disgruntled, in front of the apartment. MONA *snaps a photo.*

MONA: Cheer up. This is what you wanted!

اضحك شوي. مش هيدا اللّي كان بدّك ياه!

NASEEB: Let's go—

—يلا نمشي

They get in the car.

YARA: I was in the back seat listening to the soft music of the radio and thinking that this will be the last time I drive these roads. Ahead of us, the road forks and forks again, splitting at every avenue. The mountains rising beyond, the city thundering below, the sky—a steel blanket heavy on our bodies. I had a small backpack—and I thought this is not the first time I've lived out of a small backpack for a short time. I thought of Karam, how I left him his favourite meal on the table before walking out the door. I thought of my mother, the warrior woman, and how I lied to her and told her that I would be back soon before I kissed her cheeks for the last time. I watched the buildings streak by the window, their stones crumbling relics of a better time. And then Mona looks at me and I remember what I have always known.

كنت قاعدة ورا عم بسمع موسيقى رايقة عالرّاديو وعم فكّر إنو هي آخر مرّة بشوف هالطّرقات. الطّريق كرماله بينقصّ وبينقسم. الجبال عاليين قدّامنا، وضجة المدينة عم ترعد ورانا، والسّما متل لحاف من نحاس قاعد عأجسامنا. كان معي شنطة صغيرة—وقلت لحالي هي مش أول مرّة بعيش من شنطة صغيرة عفترة. فكّرت بكرم، كيف حضّرتلُه أطيب أكلة عندو وتركتلُه ياها عالطاولة قبل ما إمشي. فكّرت بإمي، المرا المناضلة، وكيف كذّبت عليها وقلتلها إنو ماني مطوّلة بس بِستها عخدّها لآخر مرّة. عم شوف البنايات عم تقطع من الشّباك. حجرها عتيق وتعبان بذكّر بزمن كانوا فيه الإشيا أحلى. وبتطلّع فيّي منى وبتذكّرني باللّي دائمًا قلبي عرفه.

She is my wings.

هِيّ جناحاتي.

MONA: —we drive along dusty paths and back roads—

عم نسوق عطرقات فرعيّة . . .

NASEEB: There's a crossing down here—

في تقاطع هون—

MONA: You're sure it's safe?

أنت أكيد آمن هالطّريق؟

YARA: He doesn't respond.

ما بِردّ.

MONA: Naseeb—

نسيب—

YARA: He still doesn't respond.

كمان ما بِردّ.

MONA: —we drive through a canopy of twisted trees—

—مْنِمرُق بطريق مْخَيْمة عليه غصان شجر—

YARA: —I feel the shaytans and demons baring their teeth—

—حاسّة بالشياطين والجنّ عم يطلعوا علينا—

MONA: Where are we going?

لوين رايحين؟

YARA: —he drives into the Green Line—

—بْيِقْطع عخطّ التّماس—

MONA: Why did we stop? What's going on?

ليه وقفنا؟ شو عم بصير؟

Beat.

NASEEB: Get out.

نْزَلوا.

MONA: What?

شو؟

NASEEB: Get out of the car . . .

نْزَلوا من السّيارة . . .

MONA: What's happening?

شو عم بصير؟

NASEEB: *GET OUT!*

نْزَلوا هلق!

MONA: Naseeb, what are we doing?

نسيب شو عم تعمل؟

YARA: He pulls out a gun.

بِطلِّع فرد.

MONA: Naseeb!

نسيب!

YARA: Oh God—

يا ربّي—

He is panicked, shaking, frantic, trying to keep it together.

NASEEB: What have you been doing?

شو كايْنين عم تعملوا؟

MONA: Naseeb!

نسيب!

NASEEB: I told you we had to leave—

قلتلّك لازم نفلّ—

MONA: Wait—

لحظة—

NASEEB: I only wanted to care for us, Mona. For our family.

كلّ اللّي كان بدّي ياه إنو أهتمّ فيكي منى. وبعيلتنا.

MONA: You are taking care of us! You are!

عم تهتمّ فينا!

NASEEB: The rumours . . .

الإشاعات . . .

MONA: Please wait—

بليز لحظة—

NASEEB: People were talking . . . I didn't want to believe them—

العالَم كانت عم تحكي . . . ما كان بدّي صدّقهن—

MONA: Naseeb, wait—

نسيّب لحظة—

NASEEB: And then I saw you—

بعدين شفتك—

YARA: —I have only ever known bullets and battered bodies—

—ما عرفت غير رصاص وجثث—

NASEEB: —kissing her—

—عم تْبوسيها—

He aims at YARA.

YARA: Mona . . .

منى . . .

MONA: —Naseeb, please, no, wait, please no!

—نسيب بليز، لا، انطر، بترجّاك لا!

YARA: —I don't cry—

—ما بِبكي—

MONA: You don't have to do this!

مانّك مضطر!

YARA: —I don't beg—

—ما بترجّى—

NASEEB: I do—

مْبلا، مضّطر!

YARA: —I was no longer angry, armoured, or suspicious—

—مانّي قاسية بقا. ولا قلقانة. ولا غضبانة.

NASEEB: I'm sorry . . .

سامحيني . . .

YARA: —all the decorum of our uncivil war come to play in this hour—

—كلّ شياطين الحرب الأهليّة طلعوا يلعبوا بهاللّحظة—

NASEEB *shoots* YARA *four times.*

I lie—another body—one, two, three, four bullets in my chest.

بوقَع—جثّة جديدة—وحدة، تنين، تلاتة، أربع رصاصات بصدري.

I lie . . . another body . . . eaten by the Green Line.

بوقَع . . . جثّة جديدة . . . أكلها خطّ التّماس.

YARA *dies.*

NASEEB *holds the gun steady.*

MONA *meets his gaze.*

MONA: Do it.

يلا قوِّص.

NASEEB *hesitates.*

DO IT, YOU FUCKING COWARD!

قَوِّصْني يا جبان!

He approaches MONA. *He rips the necklace from her neck.*

MONA *cries.*

NASEEB: Go back to the apartment!

ارجعي عالشّقة!

NASEEB *escapes in the car towards the mountain—he exits.*

It begins to rain.

Beyond space and time.

MONA: I laid beside you for what must have been an eternity. I saw the sun and the moon dance through the clouds and let the rain sink our bodies into the mud. I wailed and I cried—Yara—come back to me, Yara. Please, please, come back to me, please! Sleep came and went, and one night, when the moon was at its largest, I could have sworn the jinns and faeries hidden in these celestial canopies came to me.

تمدّدت حدّك لوقت كأنّو أبدي. شفت الشّمس والقمر عم يرقصوا بين الغيوم ونزلِت شتا دوِّبت أجسامنا بالوحل. بكيتْ كتير—يارا—ارجعيلي، ارجعيلي يارا. بليز بليز ارجعيلي بترجّاكي ترجعي! إجا النّوم وراح وهونيك ليلة، كان القمر فيها مدوَّر، كأنّو طِلْعولي الجنّ والحوريّات من ورا الغطيطة السّماوية.

And I begged them to bring you back. Take me and bring you back.

واتْرَجَّيْتْهُن يردّولي ياكي. خدوني إلي وردّوها.

YARA: I am cemented into the soft earth, unable to move, unable to breathe, unable to fly. I have been here, waiting, suspended in stillness.

تْزَفَّتِتْ بقلب الأرض الطّريّة، ما قادرة إتحرّك، ما قادرة إتنفّس، ما قادرة طير. إلي هون وقت ناطرة، معلَّقة بالجُمود.

Waiting for you to release me. Waiting for you to release yourself.

ناطرتِك تْحرّريني. وتْحرّري حالك.

YARA observes the following.

NASEEB re-enters.

NASEEB: I open my eyes and I am on the Green Line.

بِفتح عيوني بْلاقي حالي عخطّ التّماس.

MONA: I pray for rebirth.

عم بِدعي إخلق من جديد.

NASEEB: And as I walk through the foliage, I am naked. And I see my fists and they are claws. And I see my feet and they are sharp like talons.

عم بمشي بين الشّجر مْظلّط. بْشوف إديّي وإجريّي مخالب.

MONA: Can you hold in your heart what pain you've brought me? What tormented fragments left in my soul can't, don't, won't fight any longer? Naseeb, you carry a legacy folded in the slits of your skin and a curse that rests in your spirit. I didn't choose this war; it came knocking at my door in the middle of the night as a beautiful brown-eyed goddess. It came when her blood watered our gardens and the petals of our flowers grew like razors.

فيك تتحمّل الألم اللّي سبّبتلّي ياه؟ واللّي عمل من روحي أشلاء ما بقا بدا ولا فيها ولا رح تحارب؟ نسيب، أنت بتحمل ذنب معلِّم عجسمك ولعنة لابسة روحك. أنا ما اخترت هالحرب، هيّ إجت صوبي دقّت عبابي بنصّ اللّيل بشكل آلهة عيونها بنية. مشي دمها بجناياتنا وطلّع ورق الزّهور شفرات.

Oh, I wish I could change it!

آخ، يا ريت فيّي غَيِّر اللّي صار!

I am planted here searching for a way to have done it differently. Where could we have changed our course? You—the brother you should have been. Me, the woman I wanted to be. Yara, my Yara, with me, beyond the Green Line, beyond the mountains, the valleys, the deserts, and the seas.

انْزَرَعِت هون عم فتّش عطريقة تانية كنت عملت فيها كل شي. شو كان فينا نغيّر؟ أنت الخَيْ اللّي كان لازم يكون. وأنا المرا اللّي كان بدّي كونها. يارا، حبيبتي، معي ورا خطّ التّماس، ورا الجبال والوديان والصّحاري والبحورة.

Where could we have changed our course?

شو كان فينا نغيِّر؟

NASEEB: I swear to God, Mona, I only wanted to care for you. I couldn't, so I ran away—beyond the mountains—and I never knew what happened to you. I never finish the sale of the apartment. I left it there, for you, as it stands, overlooking the Green Line. I never knew if you went back or if you stayed amongst the plants and trees growing from the copper soil.

بِحْلِفْلِك مني إنو ما كان بدّي غير إهتمّ فيكِي. ما قدرت فهربت ورا الجبال وما عرفت شو صار فيكِي. ما رجعت بعت الشّقة. تركتلّك ياها متل ما هيّ مطرح ما هيّ بتطُلّ عخطّ التّماس. ما عرفت إذا رجعتي أو بقيتي عم تْجَذْري بالتراب بين النّبات.

MONA: You never knew if I stayed to die.

ما عرفت إذا بقيت هونيك تا موت.

NASEEB: Until all these years later, you sent me that photograph . . . and you wrote on it "Naseeb, 1978"—and all my years of forgetfulness came erupting back.

لحدّ ما بعتّيلي الصّورة بعد كل هالسّنين . . . وكتبتي عليها «نسيب ١٩٨٧» وكلّ الذكريات طلعت وفارت فيّي.

MONA: I can't absolve you of what you've done. No one can absolve you of what you've done. We can't change what's come any more than we can ask the mountains to dance. Because we are all servants to the speeding bullet of time and none of us can turn it around. So, I carry the wounds on my back and hold the scars in my fists, and I wonder if there will ever be a time when bullet shells turn to flowers.

ما فيني أغفرلك. ما حدا في يغفرلك أو يبرّيك من اللّي عملته. فينا نغيّر اللّي صار عقدّ ما فينا نطلِب من الجبال تهزّ. نحنا مش أكتر من جنود الزّمن الطّاير متل رصاصة ما قادرين نغيّرلها مسارها. فبِحمُل جروحاتي عكتافي ونَدْباتي براحات إيديّي وبِسأل حالي إذا حيجي نهار يتحوّل فيه الرّصاص لورد.

But I turned our home into a sanctuary. I stayed and you left.

بس حوّلت بيتنا لملجأ. أنا بقيت وأنت فلّيت.

NASEEB: Why did you send me the photograph?

ليه بعتّيلي الصورة؟

MONA: Because Beirut should not be forgotton, and it's not fair that you were free and I was stuck.

لأنّو بيروت ما لازم تِنتسى. ولأنّو مش عدل إنّك كنت حرّ وأنا لأ.

NASEEB: You think I was free?

كنت حرّ؟

I am so sorry, heyete. I am so so sorry.

سامحيني حياتي. سامحيني بترجّاكي.

Please, tell him what happened. Tell him everything you remember when he comes to you.

بترجّاكي، خبريه شو صار. خبريه كلّ شي بس يجي لعندك.

MONA helps YARA to her feet. NASEEB/RAMI witness.

YARA's song is heard, an echo in space, a memory. YARA becomes a spirit, unearthed and limitless.

They move through the space, in memory.

MONA releases YARA.

YARA exits.

MONA exits.

SCENE NINETEEN
A KNOCKING

2018.

The apartment.

ZIDAN enters.

ZIDAN: Where Damascus meets Independence, in the apartment overlooking the Green Line. This is where the Green Line used to run.

RAMI: It's hard to imagine.

ZIDAN: We've worked very hard to forget about it.

Is this it?

RAMI holds the photograph up to compare.

RAMI: Zidan, what if I don't like what I find?

ZIDAN: You might not.

RAMI: What would you do?

ZIDAN: I would go to the closest gay bar and get drunk with a total stranger.

They laugh.

RAMI: You're still a jerk.

ZIDAN: And you're still cute.

RAMI: Here goes nothing.

ZIDAN: Rami—

RAMI: Yes?

ZIDAN: Just remember—

When we look back, we want to believe we're better than the worst parts of us. As a place, as a people. I want to remember that my dad is the man who baked fresh bread every Sunday after church and not the man who hit the tears out of my eyes. These violent pasts don't make sense when we're always trying to convince ourselves that we are fundamentally okay. Or maybe these violent pasts remind us too much that we're still not okay.

RAMI: Memory is a funny thing—so quiet if left undisturbed.

ZIDAN: So why disturb it?

RAMI: I don't know if I have an answer to that.

> *Beat.*

ZIDAN: Will you come back, Foreigner?

RAMI: There might be something here after all . . .

> *They kiss.*

> RAMI *looks at the sign above the door, written in Arabic: Jneynet Yara.*

What does that say?

ZIDAN: Jneynet Yara . . . that's what she used to call the safehouse.

RAMI: What does it mean?

ZIDAN: Yara's Garden.

MONA enters, watching outside her window.

YARA enters, beyond space and time.

MONA: Naseeb?

نسيب؟

YARA: It's over.

خِلْصت.

MONA: That's our necklace.

هيدا العقد تبعنا.

YARA: It's over, my love . . .

خِلْصت، حبيبتي.

MONA: Yara, look.

يارا شوفي.

Beat.

YARA: You can let me go now . . .

فيكي تتركيني روح هلق . . .

MONA watches as RAMI turns to the door of the apartment.

MONA: That isn't Naseeb—

هيدا مش نسيب.

RAMI looks at her.

YARA: I'll be waiting for you . . .

حأُنطرك . . .

MONA: I think he can see us.

بعتقد في يْشوفنا.

Beat.

YARA: I'm flying, Mona. I'm flying now.

عم طير مني. عم طير.

RAMI knocks on the door.

Fade to black.

The End

ARTIFACTS OF THE GREEN LINE

I had a vision alongside this play where LGBTQ+ Lebanese artists contributed their reflections of queerness in Lebanon. This section offers poetry, images, drawings, and essays from several Queer and Trans Lebanese artists.

We are here, we will always be here.

With love,
Makram Ayache

THE PHOENIX
LEILA BALAKOS

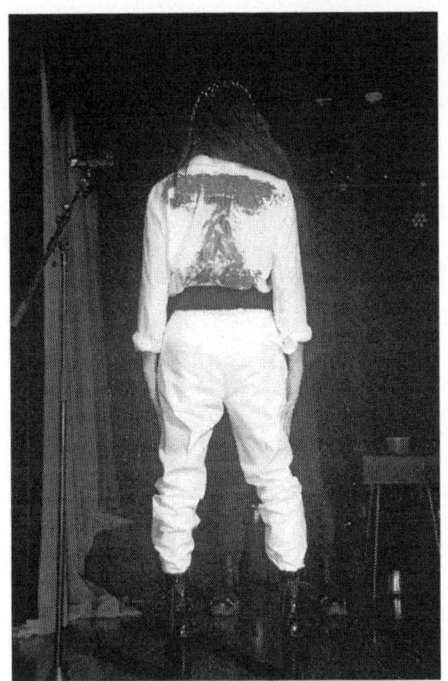

Photos by Cutline Photography from the Miss and Mr. El Convento Rico Pageant, 2023/24

Beirut, to this day, remains one of the most beautiful cities to me. What it used to be, growing up there as a child, is nicer than what it is like today. Nevertheless, Beirut has been dubbed the phoenix of the Middle East. It has been destroyed and reconstructed many times and the hope is that some day it will be alive again with the sound of kids laughing around the central clock tower, the sight of kites flying over its skies, and the smell of freshly baked ma'amoul for Eid flooding the streets. It's surreal to think that in that same little part of Beirut just a few years earlier, we also had war, suffering, and what you will come to learn in this play was the Green Line.

I was ecstatic to have been able to present all these amazing traits of Beirut, my hometown, through the character of Fifi, the Phoenix, when I played Zidan/Fifi in a production of *The Green Line*. Without spoiling too much, I was able to channel those ideas of resilience, rebirth, and reincarnation through Fifi and, subsequently, Zidan and Rami's story in the play.

One of Fifi's superpowers is drag. To see drag as anything other than a superpower would be an understatement. The amount of work drag takes, the transformation it requires, the literal rebirth of a version of ourselves we try to hide in our closets growing up (forgive the very intended pun) together create a very powerful art form that makes the people doing it seem like transcendent beings. And that is truly what drag in Lebanon feels like. Luckily, I got to witness more Lebanese drag upon visiting Beirut after I immigrated to Canada, and Lebanese drag is next-level artistry.

Being part of these amazing experiences and the deep connections to Beirut, I developed my own alternate self, a Lebanese drag personality based in Toronto, who utilizes slam poetry, elements of Southwest Asian and North African (SWANA) pop culture and belly dance, and all the camp to fight for her ancestors, fight for her people, and fight for Beirut's future generations. This is how Leila BalaKos was born.

"Leila" comes from a famous Arabic love story of Majnoun (translates to "Crazy") who was madly in love with a woman named Leila. "BalaKos," well, you probably should ask your Arab friend what this part means. In bringing the character back to life, I bring similar elements of rebirth and love in the hopes of a better Beirut.

*Leila BalaKos hails as a rising fiery phoenix in the Toronto and North American drag scene. Her name comes from the great Middle Eastern romantic tragedy of Leila and Kays. An actress, slam poet, flirty pop diva, and conceptual camp comedy queen, her credits include hosting Maziqa Party and performing for El Convento Rico, Ya TabTab Night, Habibi Nights, Hoebibi, Muslim Pride*TO*, Pride Toronto, and several other parties and venues. She also starred in her short plays* Hummus Rouge *and* Rebirth of Leila and Kays, *the latter as part of Soulpepper's Queer Cab. Outside of drag, they also are an actor, appearing in shows such as the wonderful* The Green Line. *You can follow Leila's work on Instagram @LeilaBalaKos.*

TO LARGE BODIES OF WATER, BEIRUT, AND THE ONE WHO GOT AWAY

SHAMS SEIF

No photos please
It does not sit well
With some people who love me
Every time I'm gay in a new city
I can feel my heart stretch
Room for growth
I keep mistaking
large bodies of water
For a home
Beirut is cradled in water
I grew up with sand falling through my palms

I've been coughing up sand lately,
I grew up by the sea
I want to watch the waves crash on the rocks by the seaside
by your side
I think that maybe
The small of your back
Is where countries at war
Go to heal
Where everybody
Puts down their weapons
Because the softness feels like a home
Or rain, or the sound of you
Flipping pages
Navigating the mechanics of a book
With the one hand
And holding me
With the other

And I think that maybe
Falling asleep next to you
Is the greatest kindness
God has given me

What I'm trying to say is
Kissing your belly button
Feels like
Learning a new language
What I'm trying to say is
Your belly button
Is where
The city meets the sea meets the sky
And when I kiss it
I can feel myself
Floating on water
I've been coughing up sand
I think Beirut would love you
I think Beirut would
Love you
I know Beirut would
Love you

When I think about the people I love
I sometimes forget to breathe
When I think about the cities I love
I sometimes forget to breathe
I've been forgetting to breathe
Do you ever think
About how lungs
look like
Butterfly wings?

Fly me to Beirut
Fly me to Beirut
Fly me to Beirut

I miss her streets
She is the only city
That ever housed me whole
You
You house me whole
I want to learn
All the Arabic poetry
Because it finally makes sense to me

I want to whisper
Bismillah
Into the back of your neck
Before I fall asleep

And there might be
Much blasphemy
Mixed with the poetry
Mixed with the love
Mixed with Beirut
Mixed with my bones
My skin and flesh
And scarf
And love

I pray fajr before the sunrise
Kisses your face
I make you
Vegan pancakes
And call you
Amari; my moon
We have Turkish coffee
And I don't feel
God
angry at me
I don't feel anyone
sad for me

I think if they knew
I think if they knew
How happy I am
Nobody who loves me
Wouldn't love you.

Lake Ontario
is far from being
The Mediterranean
Far from being
The Red Sea
But it is a large body of water
I could see myself
Mistaking
For a home

You
Are a large body of water
Contained
In human form
I could see myself
Mistaking
For a home
I could see myself
Mistaking you
For a home
I could see myself
Kissing you good night
I could see myself
Kissing you good morning
For a long
Long time

This poem could not have existed if not for the great love I have been afforded. You know who you are, thank you.

Shams Seif is an artist-academic, writer, and part-time nanny. They are a PhD student in Gender, Feminist, and Women's Studies and a Teaching Assistant at York University. Their research looks at transgenerational healing, as well as transgenerational trauma, from a research-creation autoethnographic standpoint. Shams values self-reflection, authenticity, and open communication. They are passionate about creating a neurodiversity-affirming learning environment and world. Lastly, they believe in standing in solidarity with marginalized communities with words, hearts, and most importantly, actions.

LITTLE BOY

SININ NAKHLE

Little boy,
you wrote your essays
as a little boy
هو**
pronouns moved your verbs
and teachers marked your words
with red flicks
and stars that stick
for the little boy
in your class book
attested only
to outstanding
—imagination

---

* Panel "إنتَ أنا؟" literal translation: "You, me?" i.e., "Are you (masculine), me?"

** "هو": he pronouns.

You are still moving, aren't you,
Little boy?

I see you in the shower
crossing over
to an image
uncut:
a mane on your chin
it has not grown
an apple from Adam
you play up in a frown
a bulge
sagging
with a handful of promises—
Little boy,
you
are not so little anymore
and I
am scared
of (dis)appearing
in your frame

Will you be good
outside the mirror
Little boy?
مش متل بيَّك
ْ و لا عنَسَق خيَّك
will you be kind
compassionate
affectionate
feminist
aware
of the masculinity
you were too hurt
to forgive in others

____

*   "Unlike your dad / different from your brother."

too elsewhere
to honour
in yourself?

Tell me, how can I,
Little boy,
long for someone
I never met
and whom
I have always been?

LET'S FUCK THE SHAME

Let's fuck the shame*
Out of our bodies
When the last call kicks in and
Barstools turn upside down

Lean against
The vitrine
Of a cheese store
As we stagger back
To our bikes
Tug on my shirt
Stare into my lip
Pull me into
Your world

---

* Title and verse 1, "Let's fuck the shame," is inspired by Mona Eltahawy's essay "Why I Say 'Fuck'" in *The Feminist Giant* (2020) referring to her declaration of faith: "Fuck the patriarchy."

I'll turn my back
To passersby
Some curious
Some giggly
Some indifferent
The rest
Imaginably violent

Let's turn an eye
Blind
To the CCTV cameras
Above our head
And pretend we are free now
Away from Beirut

We'll pass from sight
In each other's hair
Speak our tongue
Between our moans
Like this city
Was constructed
For bodies like ours
تِمّي
رَحْ إفتَحو
بَّسْ
I won't speak
Of dreams displaced or
Digital traces of protest
In my drive
Put off
Telling me
About your sister
Becoming a mother
Away from her mother
Away from you

---

*   "My mouth I will open but."

In a land too cold
To hold
The sprouting of her roots
We can channel our movement later
As we choke
On our friends'
imaginaries
About diasporic
imaginaries

Ask
Before touching my chest
To make out
The memories it binds
Grab my bulge
Like it's a dick
Let us play
With the commandments
That trained us
To kneel and
Be polite and
Never fight
For the pleasures
Of our s(k)ins
*"بُكرا بِقِولو عَنَّك شَرْموطَة"

Smear your scent
On my neck
Ride my belt
Though it might
Resurrect
The leathered whip
Of your father
When you misbehaved

---

*   "Tomorrow, they'll call you a slut."

Spoke too loud or
Spoke too soon or
Spoke at all
We'll reclaim pain
Re-wire
Re-write it
I'll ask
If I can spank you
You can show me
How hard

Sinin Nakhle is a cartoon artist, storyteller, and researcher whose work lies at the intersection of bodies, digital platforms, and protest movements. His stories around queer and trans embodiment have been featured on Netflix and in literary outlets, including the peer-reviewed academic journal Feminist Formations *and the Flemish literary magazine,* nY. *His autobiographical writings and illustrated poems have also been published in volumes alongside contributions by Fred Moten and Jasbir Puar. In 2018, Sinin created Beirut By Dyke, a webcomic series featuring short stories about being queer in Beirut. His multimedia page, which tackles intersectional topics around gender, sexuality, and mental health, came to be taught as a case study of visual ethnography at the American University of Beirut, Leiden University, SOAS University of London, the University of Chicago, and the University of Pennsylvania. Currently, Sinin is a lecturer of Global Digital Cultures at the University of Amsterdam, where he is also pursuing his NWO-funded Ph.D. on embodiment and the aesthetic activist practices of the 2019 protest movement in Lebanon.*

ACKNOWLEDGEMENTS

I couldn't have written this play without the support of Desirée Leverenz who is my trusted friend, accomplice, and director who took on the very first development production of this play in the Edmonton Fringe Festival in 2019. Her insight and clarity were a gift to the project. Amena Shehab, my dear friend, brought a cultural dramaturgy that was incised with a lived experience. She knew of my queerness and my Arabhood and held both with care and love as we developed this play. I must also tremendously thank Evan Medd, my dramaturg who helped see this play from the very early days of its development to the fullest realization. His care for story, character, and narrative guided me deeply. I thank the Major Matt Mason Collective and the Edmonton International Fringe Theatre Festival for their support in the development of this play, which helped bring the entire show to its premiere. And a tremendous amount of gratitude to Jenna Rodgers and Clare Preuss for bringing the world premiere to life. Jenna Rodgers's direction was full of care and dignity for the words, the world of the play, the real people impacted by these experiences. Clare Preuss provided for us the environment which this play came to life in during the midst of the difficult pandemic lockdown days. I also want to thank Hiba Sleiman, the beautiful artist, actor, writer, and translator, who provided the Arabic translation of this script. Working with Hiba to create the Arabic translation is the yearnings of this play coming to life. Of course, a huge thank you to my mom and dad for too many things to even begin listing here, but for their support in making the memories of this story true in my body. A huge thank you my queer kin, Josh, Brent, Kevin, and Matt, who supported me through the emotional throes of making this play a reality. And finally, the many actors, designers, stage managers, technicians, and artists that have come together to bring these characters to life across many workshops, development productions, and premieres.

Makram Ayache is a queer Arab Canadian playwright, director, and performer. He was born in Lebanon, raised in rural Alberta, and now lives between Edmonton and Toronto. His work explores representations of queer Arab voices and aims to bridge political struggles to the intimate experiences of the people impacted by them. His work is produced across Canada and aimed at creating emotional experiences that bring about lasting and nourishing social change. Ayache was named one of six breakthrough artists in Toronto by the *Toronto Star* in 2023 and is the winner of the 2021/2022 Betty Mitchell Award for Outstanding New Play. Find more at www.makramayache.com.

Hiba Sleiman is an actor, playwright, and scriptwriter who has worked internationally with renowned stage and film directors in Lebanon, Canada, and the United States. Hiba holds a double BA in Communication Arts and Psychology as well as an MA in Drama Therapy. Currently based in Montreal, Hiba translates works from French and English to Arabic and writes for the stage and screen, as well as writing poetry in both English and Arabic. Her eagerness to share her impassioned native language compels her to continuously find ways to create relevant and representational narratives through multiple languages. She wrote and created several short films and is currently developing her first full-length play with the support of the Canada Council for the Arts.

First edition: June 2024. Second printing: February 2025.
Printed and bound in Canada by Imprimerie Gauvin, Gatineau

Jacket art and design by Sam Mendoza
Author photo by Brandynn Leigh Photography
Translator photo by Eli Yabroudi

Playwrights Canada Press
202-269 Richmond St. W., Toronto, ON M5V 1X1
416.703.0013 | info@playwrightscanada.com | www.playwrightscanada.com